THE WALL STREET JOURNAL.

GUIDE TO
STARTING YOUR
FINANCIAL
• LIFE •

THE WALL STREET JOURNAL.

GUIDE TO STARTING YOUR FINANCIAL ·LIFE·

KAREN BLUMENTHAL

THREE RIVERS PRESS

NEW YORK

Library of Congress Cataloging-in-Publication Data

Blumenthal, Karen.
  The Wall Street Journal guide to starting your financial life / Karen Blumenthal.—1st ed.
    p. cm.
  Includes bibliographical references.
  1. Finance, Personal. I. Wall Street Journal. II. Title. III. Title: Guide to starting your financial life.
  HG179.B56634 2009
  332.024—dc22   2008040600

ISBN 978-0-307-40708-5

Printed in the United States of America

Design by Mauna Eichner and Lee Fukui

Illustrations: p. 6, © 2008 Peter Hoey Collection c/o theispot.com; p. 64, © 2008 Mark Stephen c/o theispot.com; p. 110, © 2008 Rafael Lopez c/o theispot.com; p. 166, © 2008 Rafael Lopez c/o theispot.com; p. 218, © 2008 Joyce Hesselberth c/o theispot.com

10 9 8 7 6 5 4 3 2 1

First Edition

TO MOM

CONTENTS

PART IV

SPENDING IT:
THE LITTLE STUFF

THE WALL STREET JOURNAL.

GUIDE TO
STARTING YOUR
FINANCIAL
·LIFE·

INTRODUCTION

Money is power. It's true—just not necessarily in the ways that you think.

Oh, sure, having millions of bucks to throw around may mean a giant house, great tables at the best restaurants, and a garage full of the coolest cars. Few of us would turn down a winning lottery ticket or the chance to switch places with Bill Gates or Donald Trump.

But having cash in the bank, relatively little debt, and an investment portfolio, even a modest one, is very powerful, too. It means you have options. It means you can probably do the things in life that you really want to do. It means that you control your money rather than your money controlling you.

If you're still in school, recently graduated, or just new to the whole money thing, you may think the decisions you are making right now involving small sums of money have little to do with where you'll end up financially. In fact, the opposite is true. The small savings you put away each month can become impressively large as you travel through life. And the small debts you accumulate can become a huge load to carry in just a few years if you don't pay them off pretty quickly.

In essence, this book gives you a navigation system for finding your way through an increasingly complex and confusing financial world. The financial crisis of 2008, still unfolding as this manuscript headed to press, only underscores the need to understand basic saving, spending, and investment strategies and put them to use early on. And while our banks and financial institutions may change and evolve in response to the worst financial problems in a century, the basics will remain the same: Careful and thoughtful money choices will pay off time and again, even when options appear limited and the future seems scary and uncertain. This book seeks to help you map out those routes so that good decisions managing your money bring you closer to your goals and bad ones don't spin out of control.

It will also help you answer questions that come at you fast and furious when you have little time to make a decision. Should you sign up for that Gap credit card just to get a one-time discount? Should your new cell phone come with a two-year contract or should you pay as you go? What is a 401(k)? What is FICO and why should you care?

Unlike many other financial guides, this book assumes you're part of the twenty-first century. That means you'll be making health-care and retirement decisions from the get-go, and considering a slew of money-sucking and money-saving services—from Roth IRAs to cell-phone contracts to exchange-traded funds—that didn't even exist a generation ago. And because you're probably as comfortable online as you are on the phone or in person, you'll want to manage your money and research your choices online as well.

With that in mind, the book takes a Mapquest approach, focusing on the most important things you need to know to find your way through more than fifty financial matters. Each chapter follows the same format, with the Map It section introducing and defining the subject, the Directions telling you how it works, and The Direct Route offering very specific and salient advice for getting the most out of the information given.

Because we all have different financial priorities, the chapters also assume there's no one right way to do anything. So, yes, it's true that giving up a daily latte habit will free up hundreds of dollars a year that could be saved or invested. But it's also true that you may really love that latte. If so, there are plenty of other ways to save a couple of bucks a day. A successful financial life is all about weighing your choices.

The hope is that this book will grow with you, starting you off on the basics of opening accounts, saving money, and shopping smart. When you're ready to start a job, it will steer you through the muddle of new-hire forms and the other intricacies of your improved cash flow. When you're ready to set out on your own, it will maneuver you through your first apartment or gym membership. When you're ready to invest, a road map to that massive subject will be waiting for you.

Once you're acquainted with your options and ready to know more, other *Wall Street Journal* guidebooks on money and investing, personal finance, real estate, identity theft, home ownership, and retirement may be useful. You'll also find shelves full of other books that offer more comprehensive details on many of these topics.

But there's plenty of time for that later. For now, you have lots of other, more fun things to do than fiddle with money. So let's make it easy and get going with "The Basics."

PART I

THE
BASICS

Once you graduate from a piggy bank, you're more or less on your own in navigating the financial world.

Sure, there are lots of friendly folks who say they will help you, but many of them are mostly eager to take your money. No one else in the financial world will care as much about what's right for you as you will. Finding the best places for your cash, learning the ins and outs of credit and debit cards, spending your money wisely, protecting your financial identity, and making careful contractual commitments will all be up to you.

Here's what you need to know most about banking, budgeting, and basic personal finance.

WHERE DO YOU WANT TO GO?

For any journey, your goals are the starting point.

MAP IT

Where are you headed? It's a simple enough question when you're going on a road trip with a clear destination. But it can seem daunting when you're talking about those bigger milestones, such as those along your career path or on the way to financial security.

Here's the good news: When it comes to your money, there are many "right" answers. And you don't need to know *exactly* where you're headed. It does help, though, to know generally where you're trying to go. Do you want only enough money to buy the newest iPod? Or are you eager to buy a car? Do you need to pay for your further education? Would you like to own a house someday?

Down the road, what are your ultimate dreams? How important is it for you to feel financially comfortable? Do you have a burning desire to be rich—whatever that means to you?

What are your goals and financial aspirations? Spend a little time thinking them through, or write them down if that

[7]

works for you. If you have a spouse or partner, talk about or write down your mutual goals as well. Once you've identified them, it will be easier to see what you need to do to get there.

DIRECTIONS

To reach your money goals, you'll need to do some advance planning. Unless you were blessed with a trust fund or won the *Survivor* jackpot, the first step toward a successful financial life will be building your savings. That means, of course, that you will have to save—and you'll have to keep from dipping into your savings to pay your bills. The more you save now, the more options and the more flexibility you will have later.

As you reach for more costly goals, you'll need to make other decisions about your comfort levels. Borrowing can help you buy big-ticket items, from a new couch or TV to a college education, a car, or a home. But each dollar you borrow is a dollar-plus that you'll have to pay back, factoring in interest payments. How much do you want to owe to someone else? How much of your earnings are you willing to give up in interest payments to others for the right to use their money? And how long do you want to be in debt?

As you reach for bigger goals, you'll also need to assess how comfortable you are with risk. Greater risks can mean greater rewards—and steeper losses. Playing poker may be fun when you're winning, but how do you handle your losses? As you make each new financial commitment or borrow additional money, consider how many other commitments you have or how much you already owe. How will you feel about those responsibilities if you lose your job or fall ill? What kind of financial cushion do you need to sleep well at night?

If you choose to put money into a savings account, your balance won't shrink, but it won't grow very fast, either. By contrast, investments in the stock market are far riskier: They can rocket up as well as slide down almost as quickly. Over time, stock-market savings should grow faster than other savings. But on any given day, or in any given month, you may actually lose money. How comfortable will you be with that? Understanding risk and your stomach for it is an important part of your planning.

THE DIRECT ROUTE

The easiest way to save is to make saving automatic and regular. Whenever you have income, whether it's a paycheck, birthday money, or contest winnings, automatically set aside some of it. A few dollars is a good start; putting away 10 percent would be much better.

If you don't yet have a checking account, see page 22 on how to open one, then start making regular transfers to a savings account. If you don't have enough money to open an account, at the least, stash your "savings" cash in a secure place away from your wallet. If saving becomes a habit, you won't miss the money and your savings will grow much faster.

Experts often recommend that you have, at a minimum, savings of three to six months of living expenses at the ready. If that seems unfeasibly high to you, then you should at least try to set aside enough to cover emergencies. Ask yourself, If I couldn't work for three months, how much would I have to pay for rent, food, and basic needs? How much money would I need to cover a big car repair or pay for a hospital emergency room visit? That's your minimum cash cushion.

FIGURING YOUR MINIMUM CASH CUSHION

Write down how much you spend on these basics each month. Then multiply the total by three, six, or twelve to determine how much you need in reserve to get by for three or six months or a year. (For more insight, see "Budgeting," page 34.)

Housing:

Rent/mortgage　　　　　　　　　　　　　　_____

Utilities (water, electric, gas, heating fuel)　　_____

Condo fees/property taxes　　　　　　　　_____

Food, transportation and other basics:

Groceries　　　　　　　　　　　　　　　_____

Telephone　　　　　　　　　　　　　　　_____

Medicine/prescriptions　　　　　　　　　_____

Drugstore basics (toothpaste, soap)　　　　_____

Car payment　　　　　　　　　　　　　　_____

Car maintenance　　　　　　　　　　　　_____

Gasoline　　　　　　　　　　　　　　　_____

Insurance:

Renter's/home insurance　　　　　　　　_____

Car insurance　　　　　　　　　　　　　_____

Health insurance　　　　　　　　　　　　_____

Other (disability, life)　　　　　　　　　_____

Debt:

Student loan payments　　　　　　　　　_____

Credit card payments　　　　　　　　　　_____

Other necessities:

_____　　　　　　_____

_____　　　　　　_____

ADDITIONAL DIRECTIONS

The CNN Money Web site has a "prioritizer" to help you resolve the inevitable conflicts between your various goals and your means, as well as good advice in its "Money 101" section. Go to http://money.cnn.com/magazines/moneymag/money101/lesson1/.

CASH

*Greenbacks, moolah, bread, dough, bills, or bucks—
cash is accepted everywhere.*

MAP IT

Cash *is* King. Almost everywhere you go, for almost everything you want to buy, you can pay cash for it.

But, duh, you already know that, right? Well, there's more.

As basic as it is, cash has a few challenges of its own. It's bulky to carry around, and if you lose it or it's stolen, it's gone. By contrast, the amount you lose from a stolen debit or credit card is limited if you report the theft right away.

If you don't have a bank account, it can be tricky to turn someone else's check into your cash.

In certain situations, you may prefer to stick with plastic and skip the green stuff. But even in an electronic world, it's crucial to have cash on hand, just in case. A natural disaster, a prolonged power outage, or even a terrorist attack could leave you unable to buy food or other basics with your debit or credit card or a check.

DIRECTIONS

If you don't have enough cash going in and out of your life to justify a checking or savings account, you may still occasionally receive checks from friends or for work you do for others. The easiest way to cash a personal or payroll check when you don't have an account of your own is to go to the bank listed on the check. (Most banks will cash checks written from their accounts.) Once at the bank, you'll need to endorse the check by signing your name in the marked space on the back exactly as it is written on the check. (Why do this at the bank? Because once a check is endorsed, anyone can cash or deposit it.)

Check-cashing stores and other outlets will cash government or payroll checks for a fee that can run from a few dollars to 5 percent of the check amount, or $25 for a $500 check. Some stores may also make you purchase a "membership" first. Wal-Mart stores will cash government and payroll checks for $3 per check, regardless of the amount.

Of course, avoiding these fees means you will keep more of your money. So, if you need to turn a check into cash only occasionally, consider asking friends or relatives with bank accounts to help you out by cashing your check at their bank after you sign the check on the back and write underneath your signature that it is payable to your friend.

If you need to pay someone else with a check, you will need to buy a money order. These are widely available at the U.S. Post Office, convenience stores like 7-Eleven, grocery stores, and some discount stores. Usually you'll pay a fee of 45¢ to $1 per money order. The money order will look much like a check with the amount printed on it. You will fill out the name of the payee—that is, the recipient—and get a receipt, which will allow you to track the money order if it is lost or stolen.

THE DIRECT ROUTE

Even if you have a checking account and a debit or credit card, keep at least $20 in cash with you all the time. With that basic amount, you'll have at least some options if you find yourself stranded with a dead cell phone. A couple of quarters can come in handy, too, just in case you ever have to use a payphone.

At home, keep at least $20—more if you're responsible for several people—in a secure place for emergencies.

When you have more than $200 or $300 in cash in your wallet and around the house, it's time to consider a savings or checking account. You'll not only have the money in a safer place, but you can also earn interest on it, which is the return that banks and others will pay you for the right to have access to your money. It's an odd concept, but having too much cash lying around can cost you because you are missing out on the chance to earn interest.

WRONG TURNS

Some banks and stores offer cards that act a little bit like a checking account but look like a credit card. Your money is loaded on these so-called prepaid cards with Visa or Master-Card logos, allowing you to pay for purchases or get cash back at stores. Generally, these prepaid cards are very expensive: You may pay $10 or more to buy one, $5 or more per month to maintain it, and an additional amount every time you add more money to it. A free checking account with a debit card is a much cheaper option. (See "Checking Accounts" on page 22.)

Resist the temptation to get cash from your upcoming paycheck with a "payday loan," a short-term loan that must be repaid when you get paid. You'll likely pay fees to the check-cashing or payday loan store of $15 to $30 for each $100 borrowed, or up to $150 on a $500 paycheck, which could repeatedly leave you short of money. If you are careful with your spending and save regularly, you will never be that desperate for cash.

Savings Accounts

The basic bank account for saving money.

MAP IT

S avings accounts are often the first step in a financial journey. They usually pay a higher interest rate than checking accounts, but are less flexible. Generally, you can't write checks on savings accounts, and you may be restricted to three withdrawals a month.

Putting money regularly into a savings account can be the best way to start and sustain a savings habit. To make it easier, most banks will let you set up automatic transfers from a checking account to a savings account.

Still, interest rates on accounts can vary widely, as do fees, and low interest rates on top of fees can be the killer combination that keeps your account from growing.

DIRECTIONS

Savings accounts used to be so easy: You made a deposit and the bank paid you a decent rate of interest, often enough to cover the annual rate of inflation, those creeping price increases that eat away at the value of our cash.

No more.

In recent years, savings accounts have morphed into a surprising array of complicated choices, with wildly different interest rates and hidden fees and costs.

Take the most basic account. If you opened one as a kid, the bank probably waived any fees or minimum amounts to encourage you to start saving at a tender age. Once you turn eighteen, however, many banks begin charging $3 or $4 a month for accounts with less than $300 or $500. At the same time, the interest rate paid on many bank savings accounts has slid well below 1 percent—to as low as .10 percent a year, or a miserly 10¢ a year for every $100 saved. That's way below the annual inflation rate of roughly 5 percent.

That means you might receive just 30¢ to $2 per year in interest on a $300 account. And if your account balance falls below $300, you could pay more than your annual interest in one monthly fee!

Still, basic savings accounts make sense if you have only a few hundred dollars in savings or if you want a backup in case you run out of money in your checking account. To avoid being ripped off by fees, keep your account balance above the minimum your bank requires.

Nearly all banks also offer money-market saving accounts. These accounts pay higher interest rates than regular savings accounts and may come with check-writing privileges, but they also may limit your withdrawals. Most money-market accounts require a minimum balance of $1,000 to $10,000. They can be convenient, since they are likely to be at the same place as your checking account. But you can probably get a higher interest rate in a money-market *mutual fund* or a certificate of deposit. (For more on these ways to earn interest, see "Better Cash Management" on page 30.)

The newest wrinkle in savings options is the online account. First offered by online banks like ING Direct, EmigrantDirect, and HSBC Direct, these accounts often have no minimum required balance and pay far higher annual interest rates, about

3 percent in fall 2008. These accounts have the fewest fees and potholes, save one: You'll never deal with anyone face-to-face. You will do all your banking—deposits, transfers, and withdrawals—electronically, by mail, or on the phone.

These accounts may be the best deal for small and large savers who are comfortable doing all their banking online. If you have a checking account, you can link the two so you can transfer money back and forth. But if you don't have another account, you will have to send deposits and get your withdrawals by the old-fashioned mail.

As online accounts have grown more popular, large U.S. banks such as Citibank have added their own higher-paying online savings accounts aimed at customers who also have checking accounts with them.

Savings accounts at banks and credit unions—even online banks—are insured. By contrast, accounts at brokerage firms—those with "Securities" in the name, even if they are affiliated with your bank—are not. Accounts at banks and thrifts are insured by the Federal Deposit Insurance Corporation, or FDIC, an agency created during the Great Depression to protect depositors. In October 2008, the FDIC raised its coverage to $250,000 per account holder from $100,000 in light of the financial crisis. That increase will expire at the end of 2009, unless it is extended. Credit union accounts are also insured up to $250,000 by the National Credit Union Association. Credit unions are not-for-profit, cooperative financial institutions run for members, like teachers, people who work for the same company, or people who live in a certain area.

The type of bank or credit union you choose is less important than the interest rate and the fees. How much do you need to open an account? How much must be in the account to avoid fees? What other charges are there?

If you start with just a little money, you can often avoid a monthly fee if you set up an automatic transfer of $25 or more from your checking account.

Because savings accounts are for savings, not spending,

withdrawals should be kept to a minimum. Some banks allow only three withdrawals per month and charge $3 for each additional one.

THE DIRECT ROUTE

Identify banks or credit unions that are convenient to your home, school, or work and check out the specifics of their accounts on their Web sites. You can also look up savings account and money market interest rates for banks in your area and online providers at Bankrate.com and Banx.com. These banks were all operating in the fall of 2008, though the financial landscape was changing. They are included only to give you an idea of the different options.

Map: Savings Accounts

Bank name	As of fall 2008 interest rate paid	Minimum to open an account	Monthly fee	Fee waived if	Other fees/ restrictions
Bank of America	0.20%	$25	$3	$300 minimum balance or $25 automatic deposit	$3 per withdrawal, after three
Wells Fargo	.05% to .20%	$100	$3	$300 minimum balance or $25 automatic deposit	$10 per withdrawal, after three
Citibank Ultimate Savings	2.25%	None	None	None	Online or phone only
SunTrust	.20%	$100	None	None	$4 per withdrawal, after two
Emigrant Direct.com	3%	$1	None	None	Online only

Now Map Your Own

Bank	Interest rate	Account minimum	Monthly fee	Fee waived?	Other fees?

In addition to doing your best to avoid monthly fees, pay close attention to interest rates. Those rates make a huge difference because of the power of "compounding," the fact that you earn interest on not only your money but also on the interest your money earns. Over time, compounding interest helps your money grow faster and faster.

Consider this example of $100 invested in two different accounts, with interest paid and compounded monthly. (For simplicity, this doesn't include the taxes you might have to pay.)

Map: How Your Money Grows
$100 Invested in Two Accounts

At the end of year	Paying 1 percent	Paying 5 percent
1	$101.00	$105.12
2	$102.02	$110.99
3	$103.04	$116.15
4	$104.08	$122.09
5	$105.12	$128.34
10	$110.51	$164.70
20	$122.13	$271.26

The *annual percentage yield*, what you actually receive over a year's time, takes into account the effect of compounding. Knowing that yield, sometimes called the APY, allows you to compare rates from one bank to another.

MAP: HOW COMPOUNDING AFFECTS YOUR RETURN

If you invested $100 at 5 percent interest:

	Annual Percentage Yield	Total after 20 years
Compounded yearly	5.000 percent	265.33
Compounded quarterly	5.095 percent	270.15
Compounded monthly	5.116 percent	271.26
Compounded daily	5.127 percent	271.81

How fast will your money grow? Use the "Rule of 72." Divide 72 by the interest rate and you'll get the number of years it will take to double your money. At the less than 1 percent rate that many banks pay on savings accounts, you'll need a lifetime—more than 72 years—to double your money. But at 5 percent, you'll double your money in about 14½ years. If you can find a way to earn an average of 8 percent per year on your money—less than the average annual return on stock investments over time—your money will double in 9 years.

The power of compounding is more impressive when you continue to add to your savings. Consider how your investments would grow if you started with $100 and added $8.33 a month, so that each year, you added another $100:

At the end of year	Amount invested (cumulative)	With 5 percent interest
1	$200	$207.40
2	$300	$320.29
3	$400	$438.96
4	$500	$563.70
5	$600	$694.83
10	$1,100	$1,458.20
20	$2,100	$3,695.17

While an extra percentage point or two in an interest rate can make a big difference in the long run, you don't need to run all over town looking for an account paying just a little bit more. Rates will change over time and one bank's lucrative interest-rate offer today may be just so-so tomorrow. You should also be wary of "teaser rates," or high initial rates that will go down within a few months. That extra thirty or ninety days of a higher rate won't do much for your money and you probably won't want to go to the trouble of moving your account once the rate goes down.

If you are comfortable with electronic banking and don't need a savings account at your bank to back up a checking account, an online account is often your best bet. Or, once you have $1,000 or more, check out "Better Cash Management" on page 30 to see if money-market mutual funds and certificates of deposit will help your savings grow even faster.

DETOUR: THE DIFFERENCE BETWEEN BANKS AND OTHER FINANCIAL SERVICES COMPANIES

The services offered these days at banks and financial services firms may seem much the same when you walk in the door. But there are important distinctions that can have a huge impact on your financial security.

U.S. banks are part of the Federal Reserve System and deposits there are insured by the Federal Deposit Insurance Corporation up to $250,000 per accountholder through 2009. Your bank accounts hold your money and may earn interest. If a bank fails, the FDIC takes over and it continues to take deposits and make withdrawals as it did before.

When a bank offers to sell you an investment, such as a mutual fund or stocks and bonds, it is doing so through an affiliate that is actually a securities firm. Securities firms and other financial services companies are not part of the banking system, but are regulated elsewhere. Unlike your bank deposits, investments generally fluctuate in value and they are not insured, even if you bought them at a bank.

The picture gets murkier when your securities firm offers an interest-paying account from which you can write checks or transfer money. Though this may seem like a checking account, it isn't. Generally, these money-market mutual fund accounts have not been insured, though that may change after the 2008 crisis. If you aren't sure about an account, ask.

Here's the bottom line as of fall 2008:

What's FDIC insured:	What's not insured:
Checking accounts	Mutual funds, including money-market mutual funds
Savings accounts	Stocks and bonds
Certificates of deposit	Annuities
Money-market savings accounts	Life insurance policies

CHECKING ACCOUNTS

The basic bank account for quick and
easy access to your money.

MAP IT

Opening a checking account makes sense when you are earning a paycheck or when you have regular expenses, such as buying gasoline, paying rent, or covering costs like clothes, food, and entertainment. Generally, you need at least a couple hundred dollars to make a checking account worthwhile. Some banks won't open an account for those younger than eighteen years old; others may require a parent to be on the account until you're eighteen.

Getting used to a checking account when you're still in school gives you practice in managing your financial affairs and helps you establish a financial identity and credit record, which could help you later. In addition, many banks offer special student accounts that may be cheaper than regular accounts.

Despite their safety and convenience, however, checking accounts can be larded with fees. Knowing the ins and outs of your account will help you get the most out of it.

DIRECTIONS

Like a savings account, you can open a checking account at a local bank branch, a credit union, or an online bank. Again, the kind of bank you use matters less than the costs and the services you get.

Most checking accounts these days come with an ATM card or debit card. An ATM card is used to get cash or make deposits at automated teller machines. A debit card works at ATM machines and also allows you to make purchases that are deducted directly from your account. While a debit card may look like a credit card (and sometimes you sign receipts just like you would with a credit card), it isn't a credit card. Instead, all transactions come directly from your account, just as if you had written a check. Most accounts also come with checks and the ability to look up your balance and pay your bills online.

With so many standard features, how do you pick the right place?

➤ If you are likely to use an automated teller machine (ATM) regularly to get cash and make deposits, start with banks that have ATMs or branches near where you live, go to school, or work. You can look up locations on the bank's Web site. Watch out for fees: Many banks will charge you $2 or more every time you use an ATM that doesn't have the bank's name on it; you'll also be charged another $2 or so by the bank that owns the ATM. That means you could spend $4 or more just to get $20 in cash.

➤ If you travel a lot or use ATMs in many places, a bank with a national presence may keep down your costs. Otherwise, look for a bank that reimburses you for ATM charges. Many online banks and some student checking accounts will automatically reimburse you for ATM fees charged by other banks.

➤ If you think you'll want to actually visit the bank regularly, consider one that is open Saturdays and Sundays or that has drive-through windows that are open into the evening.

➤ Even if you want a "free" checking account—one without a monthly service fee—you may be charged a monthly fee of $6 or more if your balance goes under a minimum amount or if you don't have a paycheck that is deposited electronically. Ask questions if you don't understand the requirements.

➤ Similarly, if you want to earn interest on your checking account, you probably will need a minimum balance of $1,000 or more all the time.

➤ If you're a student, many banks offer student accounts that don't have monthly fees. At some point, the bank may decide you aren't a student any more and simply start charging monthly fees. If that happens, call the bank and ask to convert your account to a "free" checking account, or consider switching banks for a better deal.

➤ Other fees to ask about: Will you pay a fee if you do business with a real bank teller regularly? How much will you pay for your checks? What's the charge for "overdrawing" the account, or taking out more money than you have in the account? Will you be charged for requesting copies of checks or monthly paper statements?

THE DIRECT ROUTE FOR CHOOSING A CHECKING ACCOUNT

Look on bank Web sites for a student checking account or a free checking account that fits your situation and needs. You can use the following chart to make comparing your options easier:

Map: Choosing a Checking Account

Bank name/ account	Minimum balance required?	Monthly fee?	Direct deposit required?	Limits on tellers or ATMs or phone service?	Other fees or perks?

Check out where your parents bank. Many banks will waive fees for students if their parents have accounts there.

STAYING THE COURSE

Once the account is set up, the biggest challenge is keeping track of your balance, or how much is in the account. That may seem like a no-brainer, since you can check your balance online anytime you want—but that balance on your computer screen doesn't show checks or payments that haven't yet cleared. Relying on it can leave you thinking you have more money than you have. Here's what to consider:

➤ Have you written a check that hasn't yet cleared—that is, hasn't been deposited by the person to whom you wrote it?

➤ Are all your debit-card transactions showing up? Are any automatic bill payments coming up?

➤ Is a merchant temporarily holding on to a larger amount than your purchase? To protect them from being short-changed, gas stations, for instance, may temporarily tell your bank account that your debit card purchase was $50 or more, even if you bought only $10 worth of gas. If you filled up on Saturday, your account may not be corrected until Tuesday.

➤ Are all the transactions listed actually yours, or could there be errors or fraudulent activity in your account?

WRITING A CHECK

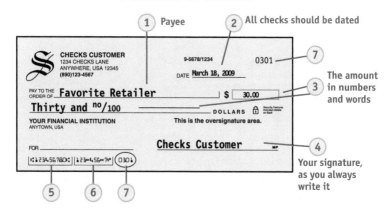

1 Payee

2 All checks should be dated

7

3 The amount in numbers and words

4 Your signature, as you always write it

5. ABA Routing Number: This nine-digit number is your check's road map through the federal banking system. The number is unique to the bank branch you use, so if you live in Pierre Part, Louisiana, and you send a check to a retailer in Penobscot, Maine, the banks involved know how to route your check back to your bank and, ultimately, your account.

6. Account Number: Your unique account number at your bank.

7. Check Number

Source: Graphic adapted from *The Wall Street Journal. Complete Personal Finance Guidebook* by Jeff D. Opdyke, copyright © 2006 by Dow Jones & Company. Used by permission of Three Rivers Press, a division of Random House, Inc.

Any of these issues could mean you have less money than you think you do and make you more vulnerable to overdrawing your account, a costly mistake. If you bounce a check, or withdraw more money than you have, you will pay $20 to $40 in overdraft fees for every transaction, no matter the size, plus additional daily fees until the money is repaid. You may also have to pay bounced-check fees to the retailer you stiffed, and your credit record could be sullied.

It's your responsibility to be sure that the deposits and withdrawals in your account are accurate. Ideally, you should write down every deposit, check, and debit-card transaction in a checkbook register or a notebook, adding and subtracting as you go along. At the least, you should save all your deposit and debit-card receipts until they show up in your online balance, to be sure the amounts are accurate. If you have a joint account, you may want one person to control the debit card and the checkbook.

Once a month, you should reconcile the balance in your checkbook with your statement. You do that by starting with your checkbook balance. Add back all the checks, debit-card transactions, and other withdrawals that haven't cleared and subtract all the deposits that haven't cleared. The amount should match the bank's balance. If that's too confusing, use the form that comes with your checking account statement to reconcile your account.

THE DIRECT ROUTE TO KEEPING YOUR CHECKING ACCOUNT ON TRACK

Okay, we know it: Realistically, you are unlikely to keep a checkbook register or actually balance your checkbook if your transactions are mostly available online. And if you write only a handful of checks a month, you may not need to balance your checkbook if you follow these steps:

➤ Check your account online regularly—at least once a month, though weekly is better—to be sure everything is correct. Let the bank know right away of mistakes or unauthorized transactions. The bank is responsible only for errors reported within sixty days of a monthly bank statement.

➤ To be sure you don't bounce a check, go to your bank's Web site to set up e-mail or telephone alerts that will automatically notify you if your balance drops below a safe amount, say $200 or $300. If you can, set up a second alert for the danger zone, say $50 or $100. When you get the alerts, you'll need to either add more money or stop spending until your next paycheck.

➤ Don't assume a deposit you made yesterday or today will be immediately available. The bank may take a couple of days—and depending on the check, even longer—to record that money as part of your account. If you deposit a birthday check and go shopping, be sure you have enough in your account *before* the deposit to cover any purchases. (By contrast, direct deposits, made electronically into your account, typically are available right away.)

➤ If ATM fees are adding up because you can't get to one of your bank's ATMs, try a different approach: When you make a purchase with your debit card at a grocery, drugstore, or discount store, take advantage of the transaction to get additional cash back. Retailers won't charge you a fee for that extra $20 or $40 like another bank's ATM will. Be sure, however, to make note of how much you are withdrawing on top of the purchase so you don't overdraw your account.

➤ If you have a bad habit of forgetting to record checks you've written, try paying your bills online. Most banks allow you to set up online bill-paying for free, allowing you to simply key in where the check should go, the amount to be paid, and when the payment should be sent. Keep in mind, though, that not all "online bills" are paid electronically. Your bank may send electronic payments to your credit-card companies and your electric company, but if you pay your rent online, for example, the bank may well write a check to your landlord and mail it for you. That transaction will be deducted from your account on the day it is to be delivered, not when it clears. You don't have to wait until the landlord gets around to going to the bank for the amount to show up in your balance.

➤ If you have both a savings account and a checking account at the same bank, be sure they are linked. (If you don't know, ask a bank representative.) If you accidentally take out more than you have in your checking account, the bank can tap your savings account for the rest. You'll probably pay a fee of $5 or $10, but it will be less than the minimum $20 to $40 fees levied for bouncing a check.

➤ If you have a joint account with a spouse or partner, have a plan for keeping track of both of your transactions. In the old days, one person had primary control of the checkbook; similarly, one person might need to have primary control of the debit card.

➤ Some banks also offer a separate overdraft protection plan that doesn't require a savings account. You may be required to pay an annual fee for the service in addition to charges every time you spend more than you have. If your bank offers "free overdraft protection," find out exactly what you'll pay; it may translate into more fees than you expect.

ADDITIONAL DIRECTIONS

This site at the Federal Reserve will fill you in further on the penalties related to overdrafts and bounced checks: http://www.FederalReserve.gov/pubs/bounce.

BETTER
CASH
MANAGEMENT

Finding a higher return for your savings over $1,000.

MAP IT

With any amount of savings, you want to put your cash to work. Once you've managed to save $1,000 or more, you'll have more options to earn higher interest rates.

For any money that you may need for the next few months or even the next three or four years, you want a low-risk account that pays the best interest rate you can find. This is where you should stash your cash for emergencies and any funds that you might tap within three years, such as a down payment for a car or the money you're setting aside for graduate school.

If you are squirreling away more than $1,000 for the longer term—that is, for at least three years from now—see Part 5: "Investing It," on page 217.

DIRECTIONS

In addition to the online savings accounts outlined on pages 15–16, there are two other safe options where you will get a higher return, or yield, on your cash: certificates of deposit, known as CDs, and money-market mutual funds.

CDs require you to lock up your money for a period of time and are issued by banks for periods ranging from three months to ten years. Most require a minimum investment of $500 or $1,000, but some require $2,500 to $10,000.

Once you buy a CD, your money will start to earn interest. But if you cash out the CD before the term expires—or, formally, before the CD "matures"—you'll typically lose a significant part of your interest. As a result, you want to buy CDs only when you're certain you won't need the money for that period of time.

Though bank CDs are FDIC-insured, these investments still carry some risk. If you buy a two-year CD and interest rates climb quickly over the next several months, you will miss out on a higher interest rate for a relatively long period of time.

Whether CDs are a good deal depends largely on current interest rates. For many years, longer-term CDs paid higher interest rates than short-term CDs and other kinds of money-market accounts and funds. But in recent years, short-term and long-term interest rates have been pretty much the same, and CDs haven't offered much advantage, if any, over more versatile short-term investments.

Your second option, money-market mutual funds, combines your dollars with those from others to invest in very short-term debt issued by the federal government, states, and big companies, aiming for the highest return with the lowest risk possible. While these short-term rates have been relatively low in recent years, funds in money-market mutual funds can be withdrawn at any time, making them far more flexible than CDs.

These funds can be purchased from a brokerage firm or a mutual fund firm. Minimum investments range from $1,000 to $3,000, though the most lucrative, highest-yielding funds may require $25,000 to $100,000.

When you buy into a money-market fund, you buy "shares"

at $1 a share, with interest paid in fractional shares. You can write checks directly out of the fund or link your mutual fund account to your checking account so that you can transfer funds electronically.

Money-market mutual funds do have some drawbacks, however. Unlike bank accounts, they aren't FDIC-insured and it is possible—though rare—to lose some of your money. Returns on funds vary from day to day, unlike a CD, which has a fixed return. That's why funds report their returns as a seven-day average yield.

The return you get from different funds can vary widely as well, mostly because mutual funds have differing levels of expenses and management fees. The fund must disclose those expenses in its "prospectus," the pamphlet it publishes describing the fund and its activities. Usually you can find the "expense ratio," or the amount of expenses deducted from the fund, posted in the fund's description on the mutual fund's Web site or at www.iMoneynet.com.

Some money-market funds focus on tax-free investments, shielding your return from federal income taxes. Because they offer a tax break, tax-free funds pay a lower interest rate than taxable investments. But tax-free funds are beneficial only if your income level puts you in the highest tax brackets. If you are in a lower tax bracket, the tax break and the interest rate combined on tax-free investments are less than what you'd earn on a taxable investment.

THE DIRECT ROUTE

In most cases, you can open a money-market fund account or buy a CD online. But read the fine print first so that you know of any restrictions.

Before you lock in your money with a CD, check out comparable rates. You can find the best CD rates nationwide and in your area at www.Bankrate.com.

If you are interested in money-market mutual funds, you should pick one that has low expenses because you'll get to keep more of the proceeds. Low-cost mutual fund families include Vanguard, Fidelity, Schwab, T. Rowe Price, and USAA. You can search for top-yielding money-market mutual funds at www.iMoneynet.com.

To choose between CDs and money-market funds, compare the rates offered. If the money-market fund rate is comparable to the CD rate, you're better off with a money-market fund that allows you to access your money at any time.

You may also want to consider whether you think interest rates will be going higher or lower over the next couple of years. If you think interest rates will go up, you may be better off in a money-market fund because your yield will go up as rates go up. On the other hand, if you think rates are going to fall dramatically, you might benefit from locking in today's yield with a CD.

MAP: COMPARING FALL 2008 RATES FOR DIFFERENT SAVINGS OPTIONS

Investment	Annualized rate
6-month CD, national average	3.16% fixed
1-year CD, national average	3.67% fixed
5-year CD, national average	4.17% fixed
Citibank Ultimate Money Account	2.65%, will vary
EmigrantDirect.com Savings Account	3.00%, will vary
Vanguard Prime Money Market Fund	2.25%, will vary
Schwab Value Advantage Money Market Fund	2.34%, will vary
ING Direct "Orange" Savings Account	3.00%, will vary
Fidelity Cash Reserves Money Market Fund	2.51%, will vary

Budgeting

Where your spending meets reality.

MAP IT

Budgets have an "eat-your-veggies" feel about them that leaves many of us wishing for dessert—or at least a shopping spree. After all, keeping track of what you earn, spend, and save can be tedious and time-consuming.

But budgets can also be liberating, helping you figure out what you can buy and when. With some attention and practice—and a willingness to make choices—budgets can show you the way to get what you really want without digging yourself into a financial hole.

On the other hand, a too-tight budget or one that tracks your money down to the penny may leave you miserable and frustrated—and ready to abandon the process at the first misstep. Relax. Just be realistic—and don't sweat the pennies.

DIRECTIONS

The first step to a smart spending plan is to figure out how much money comes in, how much goes out, and where it goes.

Start by tallying up your income for the month: paychecks, any overtime or extra income, regular gifts, and any investment income that isn't intended for savings. If you're estimating the income you will have after you start a new job, don't forget to deduct taxes first. (See "Your Paycheck" on page 74.)

Determining where the money goes will take some more sleuthing. Don't guess—you'll almost certainly forget something. Try writing down *everything* you spend for an entire month, starting with fixed expenses like your rent and car payment and moving to the irregular stuff, like shopping trips, magazines, and entertainment. Or if you use your debit card or credit card (or both) a lot, go through two or three months of statements and piece together most of your purchases.

Now consider purchases that show up less frequently: quarterly or semiannual insurance payments, haircuts, holiday gifts, clothing purchases, and necessities such as medicine or toothpaste or shampoo.

Next, group your purchases, breaking your expenses into two categories: those you absolutely have to pay (like rent or the mortgage, groceries, insurance, loans, and medicine) and those that are discretionary, like entertainment, eating out, clothes, and trips. Using all your data, calculate your average monthly expenses. Realistically, you should include some savings in the mix as well, as much as 10 percent of your income.

Are there any surprises? Are some costs far higher than you expected? If you are spending more than you are bringing in, where can you make changes?

➤ If gasoline costs are eating into your fun, could you carpool or take public transportation?

➤ If you love to eat out, could you cut back on entertainment? Or rent movies instead of going to the theater?

➤ Do you buy a lot of individual magazines? Would a subscription make more sense? Are there other items where buying in bulk would mean significant savings over buying in smaller quantities?

➤ A $3 or $4 regular habit, whether it's an afternoon snack, a morning coffee, or lottery tickets, can add up to hundreds of dollars per year, money that you might put to better use elsewhere. But if that little splurge is a highlight of your day, you don't have to give it up. Instead, find other places to save a few bucks a day, like shopping at discount stores for basics, bringing your own lunch, making dinner instead of buying prepared food, or cutting back on the nights out.

If you make living within your means your first priority, then you're on the right track to ordering your expenses to get more of what you want.

OTHER ROUTES

Relatively new online personal finance programs, Mint.com, Wesabe.com, and Geezeo.com, help you keep track of your spending and may send you alerts. Popular software packages like Quicken and Microsoft Money can speed up the math once you get them set up. Worksheets at www.WSJ.com/BookTools can help you work out a monthly budget and create a more advanced and detailed spending plan. Your online bank statement may also make it easier to track your deposits and spending.

Ultimately, though, earning and spending decisions are yours alone. If you spend too much, you'll be broke or in debt or both. It's as simple as that.

Luckily, once you've paid close attention to your expenses and other purchases for three or four months, you'll get a feel for what you can afford. Then you can probably worry less about the little details until you have a big financial decision or a crisis to resolve.

WRONG TURNS

Time and again, you'll have to decide: Do I stretch and buy a slightly nicer car than I can comfortably afford today? A better computer? A bigger house? Sure, you can probably find a way to make the purchase today and assume it will be a lot easier to pay off after that raise you hope to get next year. But at what cost? How much flexibility will you be giving up? What other purchases or savings must fall by the wayside? And what if that raise doesn't come through?

Stretching your finances too thin is a lot like buying clothes that are too small because you plan to lose weight soon. It's based more on dreams and wishful thinking than reality. Sticking to what you can comfortably afford today can avert crises and will give you far more options when your income actually does climb.

CREDIT CARDS

The simplest, most common form of debt.

MAP IT

Credit cards can seem like a form of modern-day magic: With a little piece of plastic, you can buy almost anything you want using someone else's money.

In fact, debt does have some magical properties: It allows you to stretch your current dollars to buy something you might not otherwise be able to afford. Debt may be the only way you can take part in big, life-changing experiences, like completing a college education or becoming a homeowner. But like all good magic, of course, debt—and credit cards, in particular—also has its illusions.

When you use a credit card, you are borrowing money *and* agreeing to pay at least some of it back every month. Credit cards are among the most expensive types of debt, carrying some of the steepest interest rates imaginable and a bevy of fees, because they are backed only by your good intentions. That makes the debt riskier for lenders than loans backed by an asset like a car or home—and the interest rates are consequently higher.

Still, a credit card has many benefits: It will give you more financial flexibility, especially in an emergency. You can book hotel rooms and buy online. Charging purchases and then paying for them all at once can be more convenient than writing a lot of checks. You'll get practice paying bills and you will start to build a credit history, which will be important when you want to rent an apartment, buy a car, or apply for a mortgage.

In addition, credit-card purchases come with some protection. If the merchant doesn't deliver as promised, you can hold off paying while you challenge the transaction, something you can't do if you pay with cash or a check.

But, for all the convenience and options that credit cards offer, you can quickly charge a mountain of debt that can take years to pay off. Your goal should always be to pay the full balance each month.

DIRECTIONS FOR CHOOSING A CREDIT CARD

College students may be broke and unemployed, but banks will line up on campus to sign them up for credit cards. Why? Because once they've hooked a young person, they know that customer is likely to hang around for a long time, maybe adding other accounts and loans down the road. If you're a college student who doesn't already have a credit card, you should seriously consider getting one before you graduate, because it may be easier to qualify now than when you're starting your first job.

College student or not, here's what you should look for in a card:

Flexibility. As much as possible, ignore the T-shirts, promises of money back, or other freebies that card issuers wave at you and choose the card that is most flexible and useful to you. Retailers from Gap to Amazon.com will offer you discounts off your first credit-card purchase if you sign up with them, but that's a one-time enticement. If you do all your shopping at Macy's or Target, then a credit card with that retailer might not be a bad idea. But falling for that one-time, 20 percent discount for opening a new account mostly will fill your wallet with cards that are accepted at only one chain and add to your monthly bill pile. Most people will be better off with a plain vanilla card, such as Visa or MasterCard, that is widely accepted.

The interest rate. Ignore the *teaser* rate, or the rate that applies for just the first few months that you have the card.

Focus instead on the *annual percentage rate,* or APR, the true interest rate the credit-card company will charge over a year's time. It's a tricky concept, but credit-card companies charge interest daily, not monthly. So if you owe money on a credit card, interest will compound on your interest every single day.

Here's the bottom line: If you aren't sure that you can pay off your full balance every month, a lower APR will make a big difference in how much you will pay in interest charges.

Student cards may carry APRs of as low as 14 percent and as high as 23 percent—or $23 a year in finance costs for each $100 of debt you carry. Cards with lower APRs are available for people with long, healthy credit records. Once you've established a credit record, you can call the credit-card company and ask for a lower rate.

Annual fees. Some cards offer you cash back or airline miles, but also come with an annual fee. Later on, when you have the routine down and are charging prodigious amounts, those cards may make sense for you. But for now, look for a low-cost credit card with no annual fee.

To compare credit-card offerings, check out www.Bank rate.com, www.Cardweb.com, or www.Cardratings.com and click on the "Terms and Conditions" links to get the dirty details. An easy place to start is with the bank where you have checking or savings accounts. If you have trouble getting approved for a first credit card, you have a few options. You could ask a parent or good friend to cosign with you. In

MAP: COMPARING NO-FEE CREDIT CARD OFFERS

(AS OF FALL 2008)

Card	APR/ charges	APR/ cash advances	Late-payment fee	Over-credit-limit fee	Grace period*	Default APR†
Citi Platinum Select Visa for College Students	13.99%	19.99%	$15–$39	$39	20 days	28.99%
Discover Student Card	14.99%	23.99%	$19–$39	$15–$39	25 days	30.99%
Bank of America Student Visa Platinum Plus	15.99%	20.99%	$15–$35	$15–$35	20 days	NA
Capital One Standard Platinum for Students	19.55%	22.65%	$15–$39	$19–$39	25 days	24.9%
Blue from American Express	8.99%–15.99%	19.99%	$19–$38	$35	20 days	up to 26.99%
Capital One Standard Platinum	19.8%	22.9%	$15–$39	$19–$39	25 days	24.9%
Citi Platinum Select MasterCard	8.49%–16.49%	19.99%	$15–$39	$39	20 days	28.99%

*The grace period is the time from the end of the billing cycle until the date your payment is due.
†APR charged if you are late with your payments or miss them.

doing so, they would assume responsibility if you don't pay the bill.

Another option is to start with a *secured* card, which requires you to deposit $300 or more in exchange for a credit line of the same amount. Shop around for a secured card with no annual fee, or a low one. If you pay your bills in full and on time each month, you should be able to graduate to a regular, unsecured card in about a year.

Your final option is to open a retail or oil company credit-card account so that you can charge store or gasoline purchases. As mentioned, these aren't the best cards to have because you can use the card only at the specific store or gas station. But if you use it a few times and pay off the card every time, you can probably establish enough of a credit record to get a more flexible card.

Once you have an all-purpose card, cut up the retail card. But don't cancel it, because that could hurt your credit score. (See "Credit Reports and Scores," page 47.)

STAYING THE COURSE

Once you have a card, the easy part is over. The harder part is keeping track of your spending, paying your bills on time, and avoiding extra fees and other penalties.

Whether your monthly statement arrives electronically or in the mail, take a look at the balance and the due date. In addition, make sure that all the charges are correct and notify the credit-card company immediately if they are not.

If you pay your balance in full and on time every month, you'll have free use of the borrowed money for up to seven weeks with no interest charges—from the beginning of your billing cycle until the day the bill is due. That's a sweet deal. (Credit-card companies will still make money from the fees they charge stores, restaurants, and others that accept credit cards.)

If you pay just part of what you owe, however, you will be charged interest on the remaining balance and on any new purchases. You will owe a minimum payment that includes finance charges, new fees, and at least 1 percent of your balance—a total that will equal about 2 percent to 4 percent of what you owe.

That minimum payment is truly the bare minimum. Pay only that and you could be forking over payments for this year's fun for years to come. Consider a $2,500 credit-card bill with a 16 percent APR. If you send in 4 percent of the balance every month—and never charge another purchase to the card—it will take you nearly a decade to pay it off; you would also pay almost $1,200 in interest.

Due dates will change from month to month, and paying late, or missing a payment altogether, will lead to late payment fees of $15 to $39, depending on your credit-card company and the size of your balance.

In addition, you'll pay interest charges on the amount you owe *and* the late fee. And that's only the beginning. Many companies will hike the APR they charge you if you miss a payment on their card; some companies will even sock you with a higher rate if you are late paying *another company's* credit-card bill. Late payments also can seriously ding your credit reputation. (See "Credit Reports and Scores," page 47).

Another number to watch is your credit limit, the maximum amount you're allowed to borrow, which is listed on your monthly statement. You can look at it in two ways—as how much flexibility you have or how much trouble you can get into. Ideally, the limit would be low enough to keep you out of serious debt but high enough to cover a plane ticket home or to pay for a medical emergency. See page 48 for more on how your credit limit can affect your credit score.

If you go over your credit limit, your company should simply turn down your charges—but it probably won't initially. Instead, it will slap you with another fee of up to $39. Of course, any interest charges will be assessed on that amount as well. Eventually, it will cut off your use of the card until you repay some of your debt.

If your card is lost or stolen, call the credit-card company right away. You aren't liable for charges made after a loss is reported. You also aren't liable for fraudulent charges made when you still have possession of your card. In fact, you are only responsible for the first $50 fraudulently charged to your card after it is lost or stolen, and you might get the credit-card company to waive that if you call and request it.

THE DIRECT ROUTE

There are plenty of twists and turns to credit cards, even on the easiest route, and the trickiest is figuring out your spending. For the most part, you shouldn't buy items on your charge card that you can't afford to pay for in a few weeks. If you look at your charges online regularly, you should have a good handle on how much you've spent and whether you can afford to keep charging this month.

Sometimes, you have to pay for a purchase over time. Say you have landed a new job that requires you to wear a suit every day, and you don't own any suits. Charging them makes sense—but so does figuring out in advance how you will repay the debt. When you understand the financial commitment and have a plan for it, you can ensure that you aren't still paying for those suits when you take your next job.

Here are some other shortcuts to credit-card ease:

➤ Hang on to your receipts until the charges are posted online or you get the bill to be sure the amounts are accurate. No one else will check. If you find a mistake, call the credit-card company right away.

➤ Pay your bill by the due date. If you are worried about missing the deadline, set up an automatic monthly payment out of your bank account of, say, $50, or at least enough to exceed the minimum payment. Hopefully, you'll remember each month to update it with the actual payment you want to make. But if you forget, you will at least avoid late fees.

➤ Use e-mail or cell phone alerts to remind you when the bill is due, to tell you when it has been paid, and to warn you if your charges are within $100 of your credit limit. Most credit-card companies offer a menu of e-mail alert choices that can help you stay on top of your account.

➤ Treat the minimum payment number on your bill like a typo. Pay off the balance each month, and if you can't, pay as much as you can afford to pay.

➤ If you pay your bill on time and pay a reasonable amount each month, your credit-card company may reward you with a higher credit limit. This is a mixed blessing. As you'll see later, a higher limit can help your credit score—but not if you feel like you should spend more. Think of the higher limit as a gallon of ice cream in your freezer. You shouldn't eat any more than you would with a pint. And you shouldn't eat it all at once unless you can afford the consequences.

➤ Keep a photocopy of your card, or at least a record of the number, in a safe place. If your card is lost or stolen, having the number at hand will help you report the problem.

➤ Once you establish your credit, your mailbox will be crammed with new offers. Ignore them. Better yet, ignore them and rip them up, so someone else doesn't try to get credit in your name. For most people, one credit card and a debit card are enough. At most, you need two credit cards: one for regular use and one that is solely for emergencies.

WRONG TURNS

As if credit cards didn't come with enough temptations, credit companies send out offers that look lucrative or necessary, but actually are a waste of your money.

Blank checks with your name on them encourage you to "add funds to your checking account." Tear these up, and call the credit-card company to discontinue them. Flyers promise "3 Ways to Get Cash Fast" for emergencies or just regular spending. But your credit card is not an ATM. Taking a cash advance from a credit card is hugely expensive and a terrible financial decision.

First, you'll pay a transaction fee of 3 percent to 5 percent of the balance, or a minimum of $5 or $10. Then you'll pay finance charges from the date of the advance at annual rates up to 25 percent. To extract even more fees, many companies then require you to pay off your balance for credit-card purchases *before* you pay off the cash advances. You could easily pay $60 in interest and other charges for a year's use of $200. The only reason to incur such costs would be a true emergency.

Another solicitation you'll often find in your monthly credit-card bill is for credit-protection insurance that will allegedly cover your bills if you are ill or disabled. This insurance is relatively costly and it doesn't cover very much; toss the offer.

VEERING OFF THE ROAD

Despite our best efforts, we all make mistakes, whether it's forgetting to pay a bill or getting carried away with spending on vacation.

In credit as in life, little mistakes are easier to resolve than big ones. If you miss a payment, pay it as soon as you can. If you are less than thirty days late, the mistake isn't likely to hurt your credit record. You should also call your credit-card company and ask for leniency. The first time, at least, it might be willing to waive the late fee or reduce it.

If you know you cannot make a payment, call the credit company, briefly explain your situation, and offer a reasonable plan for fixing it. Many companies will work with you because they want to get paid, and they'd rather that you fess up than hide out. It's in their interest, as well as yours, to work out a resolution.

If you've dug a really big hole, not-for-profit agencies can help you figure out what to do. Many college campuses have financial counseling offices. Many communities have not-for-profit Consumer Credit Counseling Services (CCCS) or Money Management International (MMI) offices. Or look for an agency affiliated with the National Foundation for Credit Counseling (NFCC). Counselors there will help you work out a plan to repay your debts.

CREDIT REPORTS AND SCORES

How lenders and other financial companies rate you.

MAP IT

Sorry to break it to you, but you'll keep getting grades long after you leave school—only this time, you may not know what they are.

Three main credit bureaus in the United States keep close track of your credit cards, loans, and other debts, including whether you pay on time and how often you sign up for new credit.

Based on that data, another company, Fair Isaac Corporation, has created a so-called FICO score, which attempts to reflect how much risk a lender takes when it lends to you. Because each bureau collects slightly different information, you will have three different FICO scores, though they should be pretty similar.

When you apply for a new credit card or a car loan and sometimes when you apply for a job, lenders or employers may check your credit record and your FICO score. The better your score, the less interest you'll pay on your debt.

DIRECTIONS

Your FICO score is a number, ranging from a low of 300 to a high of 850, based on a mix of information:

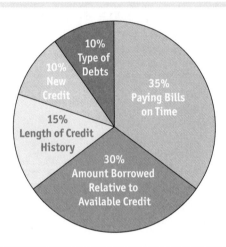

➤ Do you pay your bills on time? This answer determines about 35 percent of your score. Recent late payments will hurt your score more than older ones. Payments that were more than ninety days late will hurt more than one payment that was thirty days late. A single late payment on one account won't ruin your score, but it could stay on your report for several years.

➤ Are you borrowed to the max? The amount you have borrowed relative to the credit you have available accounts for about 30 percent of your score. If you have a $1,000 credit limit, for instance, but rarely carry more than a $100 balance, lenders will think you're using your debt prudently. If you want to improve your credit score, you should try to reduce your debt to 10 percent or less of your credit limit. If your lender raises your credit limit and you don't borrow any more than usual, you might help your credit score. This factor is one reason experts recommend that you leave unused accounts open—it will suggest you are smart about how much debt you use.

➤ How long have you had your credit cards or mortgage loan? The length of your credit history contributes about 15 percent of your score. That's another reason to keep older accounts open, even if you aren't charging on them anymore. The longer you have successfully borrowed money and paid it back, the less risk you are to a lender.

➤ Are you cautious or aggressive about signing up for new credit cards and other debt? About 10 percent of your score will be based on whether you've been snapping up new credit in the last year. The score will factor in how many accounts you have, how long it has been since you got a new account, and who is inquiring about your credit. But don't worry if you're, say, shopping for a car loan or a mortgage; similar inquiries made within a two-week period won't hurt your score.

➤ What kind of debt do you have? The last 10 percent of your score comes from the specific mix of debt you owe. Are you knee deep in credit-card payments? Or do you have a reasonable mix of a car loan, student loan, and modest credit-card debt?

In deciding whether to loan you money, lenders may consider aspects other than your FICO score, including your income, your job history, and assets such as the money in your bank account. But a good FICO score can make a huge difference in what you pay. Consider the cost of a four-year loan for a new, $27,000 Toyota Prius in 2008, according to the Toyota Web site:

Map: How Your Credit Score Affects Your Borrowing

Financing a $27,000 Prius for 48 months

Credit quality	FICO score	APR	Monthly payment	Total cost	Difference over four years
Excellent	720+	6.4%	$639	$30,672	
Great	690–719	7.3%	$650	$31,200	$528
Very good	670–689	8.5%	$665	$31,920	$1,248
Good	650–669	10.3%	$688	$33,024	$2,352
Fair	630–649	13%	$724	$34,752	$4,080
Poor	610–629	14.7%	$747	$35,856	$5,184
Very poor	580–609	18%	$793	$38,064	$7,392

THE DIRECT ROUTE

Once you have credit, checking your credit reports once a year is a good habit. Errors can creep in that may hurt you down the road, and occasionally identity thieves may steal your personal information and open credit in your name without your knowledge. (See "Avoiding Identity Theft," page 53.)

Credit bureaus are required by law to provide you with one free credit report a year. This doesn't include your FICO score, but lists your credit cards, loans, and other debts. You can look at one bureau at a time, or all three, by going to www. AnnualCreditReport.com. If you worry about identity theft, you can spread out your free reports, checking a different one every four months. That's much cheaper than paying for extra credit reports, which run $10 or more.

In addition, if you are turned down for credit, you are entitled to a free copy of your report and an explanation.

After you review your credit report, contact the individual credit-reporting company if you see a problem with the information:

➤ Experian: www.Experian.com, 1-888-397-3742

➤ Equifax: www.Equifax.com, 1-800-525-6285

➤ TransUnion: www.Transunion.com, 1-800-680-7289

The company must respond to your letter or e-mail within thirty days, so keep track of all your correspondence.

To actually see one of your FICO scores, you'll have to pay about $15, or about $45 for all three scores. It's helpful to check at least one score in the months before you need a car loan or a mortgage so that you'll know where you stand. If your score isn't what you expected, you might want to delay your purchase until your credit is in better shape, saving you lots of money in the long run.

Improving your score takes two things: time and common sense. Some serious problems, like defaults, can take up to seven years to overcome, while other issues, like high balances, can be resolved in a matter of months. If you pay your bills on time and keep your debt levels modest, your rating should take care of itself.

WRONG TURNS

A few seemingly innocent moves can hurt your score or cost you more than necessary:

Furniture and electronics stores like to entice buyers to make big purchases with promises of "no interest for six months" or "no payments until next year." Sometimes these are set up as installment loans, like a car loan. But more commonly today, they are simply a credit-card offer with the interest or payments delayed.

That means you have yet another credit card on your record. In addition, your credit limit in these situations may be just the purchase price or perhaps a little bit more. So this new credit will show up as maxed out or close to it. If you pay it off slowly to take advantage of the no-interest or no-payment offers, it may look like you're racking up the debt, which could hurt your credit score.

Ultimately, these offers don't save you very much money and may not be worth the risk they could pose to your credit score.

Similarly, don't sign up for retail cards just to get the discount or apply for credit just to see if you can qualify. The more credit you line up, the more it may look like you're ready to binge, hurting your overall ranking.

Finally, ignore the hard sell from credit bureaus and My-Fico, a Fair Isaac service, to pay for ongoing services that give you daily access to your credit reports or scores. These services are relatively expensive and unnecessary. You only need a general sense of your score, not a day-by-day report.

ADDITIONAL DIRECTIONS

The Fair Isaac Consumer Web site, www.MyFico.com, has lots of additional information about credit scores under Credit Education. Just ignore the offers to constantly track your score.

Avoiding Identity Theft

How to protect your good name.

MAP IT

Once you become the proud owner of a debit card or credit card, you might as well have a target painted on your back. Some crook is always looking to take advantage of your carelessness to get something for nothing.

The hardest part may be realizing that these kinds of thieves aren't always strangers. Cash-strapped roommates have swiped credit-card solicitations and run up thousands of dollars in bills in their roommates' names. Sometimes, creeps have used the Social Security numbers of friends, relatives, and coworkers to open bank accounts, get credit cards, or get cash from an existing account.

While you can't completely avoid the clever and determined wiliness of credit-card or identity thieves, you can take precautions to help deter them.

DIRECTIONS

The good news, as mentioned earlier, is that your financial liability should be limited if you notify your bank or credit-card company as soon as you notice something amiss. That means vigilantly watching your accounts for signs of fraudulent activity.

But the bad news is that straightening out fraudulent charges and getting reimbursed can be a huge headache.

For starters, you'll lose the use of any missing cash until the bank actually reimburses you. Credit-card issuers will instantly cancel your card, and you'll have to wait for a new one to arrive. Then you'll have to contact those who charge you monthly and update any places where your credit-card information is automatically stored.

The best way to be alert for fraud or identity theft is to pay attention: Check your credit-card and bank statements online at least once a month for any unusual activity—weekly would be better. And check your credit reports once a year—or once every four months—to be sure someone hasn't used your information to open new credit lines.

THE DIRECT ROUTE

In addition to keeping an eye on your accounts, here are some other rules of thumb to protect yourself:

➤ You might share your deepest secrets with your best friends, but don't share your personal identification numbers, or PIN numbers. Make them complex enough that someone who knows you casually couldn't guess them.

➤ Keep your checks in a safe place, not on the kitchen table. If you rarely write checks, you might want to actually hide them in a secure spot.

➤ Thieves have been known to steal credit-card bills from mailboxes and then change the address to their own. Then they will run up charges under your name—but you won't know about them. Be sure any change of mailing or e-mail address is accurate. If you haven't received a particular bill in a while, call the issuer to check on it.

➤ Phishing, or sending e-mails that look just like bank, retail, or PayPal e-mails, is one way crooks try to get you to divulge your information. Your bank and credit-card company will never solicit your account numbers or password from you online or over the phone. But to be certain they won't, don't click on a link from an e-mail; instead use your Web browser to go directly to the site.

➤ Never give out or type in your credit-card numbers, PINs, or passwords in response to unsolicited phone calls or e-mails.

➤ Cut up any old credit cards that you have stopped using, even if you are keeping the account open to enhance your credit score.

➤ Never save your online ID or passwords on a computer at school, a library, the office, or other place where people outside your family have access to it.

ADDITIONAL DIRECTIONS

The Federal Trade Commission Web site at www.FTC.gov has pages of information about identity theft and what you can do about it.

For a thorough reference, consult *The Wall Street Journal. Complete Identity Theft Guidebook.*

CONTRACTS

What to consider before signing on the dotted line.

MAP IT

Cell phones, health clubs, apartments, jobs—it can seem like everyone wants you to make a lengthy commitment by signing a contract. But legal documents and agreements can be tricky, with unpleasant terms hidden in the fine print.

Worse, there are serious consequences if you can't keep up your side of the deal. Creditors can hound you, your credit score can dive, or you could find yourself in an expensive and time-consuming lawsuit.

Knowing and understanding the terms and consequences before you sign can keep you from contract nightmares.

DIRECTIONS

Unfortunately, you really do need to read a contract before you sign it, especially if you're making a commitment that will last a while.

Rather than trying to figure out where lawyers found all those big words, consider the exercise something of a scavenger hunt. This is what you're trying to find:

➤ What you will pay (or be paid) and when.

➤ How long the contract will last.

➤ What the penalties or consequences are if one side doesn't stick to the agreement.

➤ How the contract ends. Does it automatically renew or have to be renegotiated? If renewal is automatic, how can you stop it if you don't want it?

➤ Other ways you can end the contract. For instance, do you need to give sixty days' notice or pay a penalty to end the contract early? And how can the other party get out of it?

➤ What limits, if any, the contract puts on you.

THE DIRECT ROUTE

Once you've answered the basic questions, you may feel ready to sign. But here are a few other ways to protect yourself from difficulties later:

➤ If you don't understand any terms, ask questions. Once you sign, you're committed, and there's usually no going back.

➤ Be sure the terms in the contract match any handshake agreement you have. Is the salary in an employment agreement the same as what was promised? Is the monthly payment what you were told it would be?

➤ Make sure all of the blanks in the contract are filled in, so that someone can't make changes without your knowledge.

➤ Most contracts are negotiable, so don't hesitate to ask for different terms. Any changes, however, need to be put in writing and agreed to by all the participants in the contract. Terms that are not written can be very hard to enforce.

➤ You should be able to take a contract home and read it at your own pace rather than feeling pressured to sign on the spot. Ask someone you trust, such as a friend or family member who has had experience with this kind of contract, to take a look.

➤ Understand the consequences. Some employment agreements, for instance, may prevent you from leaving to work for a competitor or may restrict your job options later.

➤ If the term seems long, it probably is. Health clubs may want you to sign up for two or three years, but that's a long and costly obligation for a young person whose lifestyle may change in a few months. Salespeople may try to pressure you into a longer relationship than you want. You shouldn't agree to anything that feels uncomfortable.

➤ Your state may allow you to change your mind about some contracts within three business days of signing. To know your state laws, check your state's consumer protection or attorney general Web sites.

➤ Make sure you have a copy of any contract you sign.

PAPERWORK

The stuff you need to keep.

MAP IT

Monthly statements, pay stubs, bills, warranties, receipts, medical and health-insurance records—life today generates a stunning amount of paperwork and electronic record keeping.

Most of us are tempted to either save everything until the piles threaten to topple over and crush the cat, or toss everything and risk losing an important document.

For the most part, there are only two reasons to save records and other paperwork: if you need them for your tax filings and if you need them to prove that you paid something or to document an event.

Keeping organized is a real hassle and, admittedly, a chore. But having the right documents at the right time will save you lots of future headaches.

DIRECTIONS

Let's start with the inevitable: taxes.

The Internal Revenue Service can audit you for any reason within three years after a tax return is filed and within six years if it believes you underreported your income by at least

25 percent. (There is no time limit, however, if fraud is involved.) So you need to keep any tax-related records at least three years, and longer if you're self-employed.

What does that include?

➤ Any year-end tax records, like W-2 statements of your earnings

➤ 1099 forms that show how much you received in dividends and gains on investments

➤ Bank-account tax forms showing interest you earned

➤ Student loan or home mortgage documents showing how much you paid in interest

➤ Records of property taxes, state taxes, and other taxes you pay

➤ Receipts for charitable contributions

➤ Receipts for medical expenses, if they were large

➤ Receipts for work-related expenses if you're self-employed or if they were large

➤ Receipts for purchases and sales of stocks, bonds, or mutual funds and any contributions to retirement accounts. When you buy any investment, keep the purchase receipt in a safe place. You'll need proof of what you paid for the investment when you sell it.

➤ Credit-card statements that show business expenses or charitable contributions

Other financial documents that you should keep:

➤ Bank statements going back at least three years, either on paper or electronically in a file on your computer. You may need them for tax purposes. And every once in a while, you may need proof that a check was paid, for instance, so that you can be reimbursed for health-care costs

➤ A single sheet with all your student loan information: the name, address, and phone number of each lender; the amount borrowed; and when the first payment is due

➤ Warranties and instruction manuals for big-ticket purchases, like televisions and computers, as well as receipts for high-dollar items including furniture or mattresses, which may have a long warranty

➤ Insurance policies

➤ Car records, including repair receipts

➤ Receipts for major home improvements

THE DIRECT ROUTE

Pick your poison—file folders, large envelopes, different colors of pocket folders, or whatever filing system you'll stick with.

Make one file for this year's tax documents and receipts. Make another for home expenses and another for insurance policies, and so on. Put away documents as they come in, or at least once a month. Otherwise, the paper stacks can grow to frightening heights.

While you're at it, make a one-time personal file. Make a copy of your driver's license, passport, immunization records, credit and debit cards, insurance cards, and Social Security card. If you ever lose any of those, having a copy can make replacing them much easier.

PART II

EARNING IT

Regardless of your career aspirations, you'll know you're on your way when you become a taxpayer. That's the funny—and sad—fact about earning money: As soon as it starts to come in the door, it also heads out.

The challenges of managing your paycheck go beyond simple budgeting. Before you start a job and from the first day of work forward, you'll be making decisions about your well-being along with your money. Where and how will I live? What kind of health insurance do I need? What will my lifestyle be? And do I really have to think about retirement before I've made a dent in my student loans?

How you weigh and balance those decisions will affect how much money you have now and later to spend on the things you really want.

The Hidden Costs of Working

The expenses start before the job does.

MAP IT

A new job can be hugely expensive, especially if you are planning to relocate.

You'll need cash for a rent deposit or maybe a down payment. You may need to buy a car or adjust for new commuting costs. You may need a new wardrobe. And even if you're lucky and your new employer is paying the moving costs, you may have to foot the bill up front and wait for reimbursement.

To avoid beginning your new life in a financial hole, it helps to have some ideas about what to plan for and how.

DIRECTIONS

Even before you accept a job offer, start considering the up-front costs:

> ➤ Where will I live? How much will it cost to rent a place? (See "Renting an Apartment," page 124.)

➤ How much will moving cost?

➤ Will I need a car? If so, what will parking cost? How much will I spend on gasoline and insurance?

➤ If I use public transportation every day, how much will that cost?

➤ What kind of clothes might I need?

➤ Will I pay state and local taxes, on top of federal taxes? (See "Your Paycheck," page 74.)

➤ What will must-have benefits, like health insurance and disability insurance, cost me?

THE DIRECT ROUTE

Preparation can make the transition to a new position less painful. For instance, assume that your new paycheck won't arrive the first week. In fact, depending on how often your employer pays, you may not get a real paycheck for two or three weeks.

Some employers may be willing to give you an advance on your first check to ease the wait. Even so, you may need some extra cash to bridge the gap before that first check—so save up a little in advance or transfer some extra funds into your checking account from your savings so that you're covered.

Some new jobs may also require decent office clothes. You may want to wait to see how your coworkers dress and how the office thermostat is set before investing in a whole new wardrobe. But you might also want to start asking for work clothes or retail gift cards for your birthday and other holidays so you'll have something other than jeans and T-shirts to wear the first week.

When you're hired, ask your employer for a copy of the employee benefits handbook so that you can get familiar with the options before you face that pile of paperwork on your first day. To better understand how to handle all that paperwork, keep reading. The following chapters will take you through the process.

Summer Internships and Jobs

MAP IT

For many, summer jobs and internships have become ever more important for finding employment later. Trouble is, many of these jobs offer experience but little or no pay. And the internships may be in places such as Washington, D.C., or New York City, or far from home or school, making short-term living arrangements expensive and challenging.

DIRECTIONS

Given that you have to eat and have a place to sleep, you will have to decide if you can afford to take a low-paying or non-paying internship. If you're a student on financial aid and your college expects you to earn a certain amount over the summer, ask the financial aid office if it will waive the requirement so that you earn job experience.

A few schools have grants or stipends for internships or may know of available money. Check with your career office. You may also have to consider a second, paying job working nights and weekends to make ends meet.

Some internships require that you receive school credit as a condition of employment. If your school doesn't give credit for internships, sometimes a letter from your department or the career office saying so will suffice. But if you have to get credit and can't, or if you have to pay a few thousand dollars in private-college tuition to work for free, consider signing up for an internship course at a community college instead, where tuition may be modest. Even if the credit doesn't transfer, you'll still gain valuable knowledge, and you might save hundreds or even thousands of dollars.

The other major financial consideration is housing, for which the cost can be daunting, especially in big cities. One option is to see if alumni from your school will put up students for the summer. Another may be universities in the area that rent dorm rooms—and provide cafeteria services—to other students in the summer. Dorms are convenient, and they might be cheaper than renting or subletting a furnished apartment.

You can also check out Craigslist for possible places to sublet and for roommates. Look on your school's career Web site for additional ideas. Rutgers (careerservices.rutgers.edu) and Berkeley (career.berkeley.edu/Internships/IntHousing.stm) have particularly good listings of Web sites with summer housing leads nationwide.

THE W-4

The evil form that starts the tax-paying process.

MAP IT

It's only two pages long, but this dastardly form can make you think twice about working. Because the government doesn't want to wait until April to get its tax money, we pay as we go, meaning federal income taxes are withheld from each paycheck. The goal of the W-4 or "Employee's Withholding Allowance Certificate" is to help your new employer figure out how much.

Unfortunately, because our tax laws are complicated, the W-4 can feel pretty complex, too.

It's important to understand it, though, because how you fill out this form can have a big impact on your paycheck and your bank account. Withhold too much in taxes every week and the government gets free use of your money until you get your refund check next year. Withhold too little and you'll have a nasty tax bill to pay in the spring.

DIRECTIONS

The W-4 is usually the first thing you fill out when you get a job. To get started, take a deep breath and fill in your name and ad-

Cut here and give Form W-4 to your employer. Keep the top part for your records.

Form **W-4**	**Employee's Withholding Allowance Certificate**	OMB No. 1545-0074
Department of the Treasury Internal Revenue Service	▶ Whether you are entitled to claim a certain number of allowances or exemption from withholding is subject to review by the IRS. Your employer may be required to send a copy of this form to the IRS.	2008

1 Type or print your first name and middle initial.	Last name		2 Your social security number
Home address (number and street or rural route)		3 ☐ Single ☐ Married ☐ Married, but withhold at higher Single rate. Note. If married, but legally separated, or spouse is a nonresident alien, check the "Single" box.	
City or town, state, and ZIP code		4 If your last name differs from that shown on your social security card, check here. You must call 1-800-772-1213 for a replacement card. ▶ ☐	

5	Total number of allowances you are claiming (from line **H** above **or** from the applicable worksheet on page 2)	5	
6	Additional amount, if any, you want withheld from each paycheck	6	$
7	I claim exemption from withholding for 2008, and I certify that I meet **both** of the following conditions for exemption.		
	● Last year I had a right to a refund of **all** federal income tax withheld because I had **no** tax liability **and**		
	● This year I expect a refund of **all** federal income tax withheld because I expect to have **no** tax liability.		
	If you meet both conditions, write "Exempt" here . . . . ▶	7	

Under penalties of perjury, I declare that I have examined this certificate and to the best of my knowledge and belief, it is true, correct, and complete.

Employee's signature
(Form is not valid
unless you sign it.) ▶ _____   Date ▶ _____

8 Employer's name and address (Employer: Complete lines 8 and 10 only if sending to the IRS.)	9 Office code (optional)	10 Employer identification number (EIN)

For Privacy Act and Paperwork Reduction Act Notice, see page 2.   Cat. No. 10220Q   Form **W-4** (2008)

dress in the right spots on the bottom of the first page. You're almost halfway there!

If you can't deal with the nitty-gritty details, skip down to **The Direct Route,** but if you really want to understand your W-4, keep reading.

After you fill in the basics, you need to fill in your total number of personal allowances on line 5. That's the real giant-killer, the number that affects whether a little or a lot is taken from each paycheck for taxes. (Personal allowances is a tax term that determines how much of your pay is exempt from tax-withholding.)

To figure out what to withhold, you will pick from three different worksheets. The one on the first page, Personal Allowances Worksheet, primarily addresses how many people are in your household and how many jobs they have. The top worksheet on the second page tries to account for any tax deductions or adjustments you may have, like interest on student loans, contributions to charities, and home-mortgage interest. And the last worksheet addresses two-earner couples or those with more than one job.

What difference does it make? Let's assume you are single, have only one job making $40,000 a year, and your employer pays you every other week. Here's what your withholding would look like in 2008 depending on how many allowances you put on line 5:

Allowances taken	0	1	2
Withholding per paycheck	$222	$188	$159
Annual withholding	$5,772	$4,888	$4,134

If your taxes are very simple—that is, you have no other income and no deductions—you would owe about $4,256 in taxes. Taking two allowances would put you closest to that number—but you would owe the IRS about $120 on April 15. If you chose one allowance, you would get a refund of more than $600 instead. That would probably be a windfall, but it is also money you could have invested and earned interest on had you claimed two allowances.

THE DIRECT ROUTE

The easiest way to figure your withholding allowance is to go to the IRS Web site at www.IRS.gov, click on the tab "Individuals," and click on the withholding calculator. If you have already worked during the year, you'll need a paycheck stub to help answer all the questions. The calculator will estimate both your withholding and your taxes, adjusting, for instance, if you start a job late in the calendar year.

If even the withholding calculator feels too overwhelming—and a new boss is hovering over you while you fill out the form—put down 1 on line 5 if you are single with one job. You might be withholding too much, but you can update it later when you have a better handle on your taxes.

Don't forget to sign and date the form before you turn it in.

If you start a job in the summer, you can write a letter to your employer asking that it use the "part-year method," which adjusts your withholding to reflect that you'll earn, say, closer to $20,000 than $40,000 for that calendar year.

ADDITIONAL DIRECTIONS

You can adjust your tax withholding anytime you want. If your refunds or tax payments are larger than you like, you may want to recalculate your withholdings. If your earnings change dramatically, you can also revisit how much is withheld.

And if your life changes—if you relocate, buy a house, get married, or have a baby—you definitely should recalculate your withholding.

Knowing your own situation can help you make adjustments without a lot of extra work. For example, if you have substantial dividend or interest income, which isn't taxed as you go, you should choose a lower number of allowances and withhold more. If you don't have any other income but pay interest on student loans, select the higher allowance number and withhold less.

In any event, don't make up a number or try to avoid withholding altogether without a good reason. Eventually, the IRS will catch up with you.

YOUR PAYCHECK

It's never as much as you hope it will be.

MAP IT

It's a rotten reality of life: You agree to a decent salary or hourly pay rate and get to work. You begin to count your earnings in your head. Then payday comes, and the check is . . . terribly disappointing.

Where does it go? Taxes, mostly: federal taxes, state taxes, Social Security, Medicare, and sometimes city taxes. Beyond that, you almost certainly will pay for at least part of your benefits, which can include health insurance, life insurance, disability insurance, and contributions to your retirement account and to accounts that help with your medical costs.

When all is said and done, as much as 35 percent to 40 percent of your paycheck could be gone before the deposit hits your bank account.

DIRECTIONS

Most employers will directly deposit your paycheck into your bank account. If that option is offered to you, take it. It will save you regular trips to the bank or ATM, and many banks will waive monthly fees if you have direct deposit. Besides, direct deposits, unlike checks, can't be lost or accidentally sent through the wash.

You already know that your federal tax withholding will depend on how you fill out your W-4, but there is one big exception: Bonuses, or other supplemental income, typically are subject to withholding at a higher rate. Companies have a couple of options for withholdings on bonuses, but many simply withhold a flat 25 percent. In other words, if you receive a $1,000 bonus, the company may withhold $250 for federal taxes and *then* take out Social Security, Medicare, and other payroll deductions.

While federal and state income tax rates vary depending on how much you earn, the withholdings for Social Security and Medicare are the same for everyone. If you work for a company, 6.2 percent of your earnings will go to Social Security taxes, which sometimes will show up on your check as OASDI— for Old-Age, Survivors, and Disability Insurance. Another 1.45 percent of your earnings will go to Medicare taxes. Occasionally, one or both may show up on your check as FICA—for the Federal Insurance Contributions Act.

While 7.65 percent of your pay may seem like a lot for government benefits that may never benefit you, that's not all they cost. On your behalf, your company will match your contribution to Social Security and Medicare. If you are self-employed, however, you will pay the full amount—15.3 percent of every dollar you earn—for Social Security and Medicare.

If you make an impressive income, you may actually reach the annual maximum on Social Security taxes. In 2009, Social Security will be applied to the first $106,800 earned, an amount that has been going up every year. There is currently no income limit on Medicare taxes.

Additionally, most companies now expect employees to pay for at least part of their medical and dental insurance, typically about 20 percent of the total cost of the insurance. Depending on the plan you choose and whether you are married and have children, that amount can range from a few dollars to hundreds of dollars a month. (For more details, see "Health Insurance," page 78.)

Finally, if you want to have any money to retire on, you'll probably need to contribute to a retirement plan, often called by one of several legal names, depending on the type: 401(k), Individual Retirement Account (IRA), 403(b), or Keogh, among others. Many of these retirement contributions can be made before taxes are taken out, cutting your annual tax bill.

Other possible paycheck deductions:

- ➤ Parking
- ➤ Use of a fitness center
- ➤ Flexible spending accounts
- ➤ Day-care services
- ➤ Payments to buy company stock
- ➤ Contributions to United Way or another charitable group
- ➤ Union dues

THE DIRECT ROUTE

There aren't many easy solutions here—just some solid advice: If you can save on taxes, consider it.

For instance, if you contribute $100 a paycheck to a 401(k) account, you won't pay federal or state taxes or Medicare or Social Security on that $100. You will be putting away money for your future and saving on taxes today.

Some companies allow you to pay for health insurance pretax. Other tax savings can come from:

- ➤ A medical flexible spending account, which allows you to put money away each year tax free to help with medical or dental costs
- ➤ A health savings account, a different kind of account to help with medical costs

➤ A dependent-care flexible spending account, which can help with child-care costs or care for elderly parents

Sometimes, you can even pay for parking and other transportation needs before taxes.

All of these can make figuring your take-home pay an exercise in advanced math. With so many possible deductions nibbling away at your earnings, don't spend that paycheck till you see it. There may not be as much there as you expect.

HEALTH INSURANCE

You need it no matter how healthy you are.

MAP IT

Like all insurance, health insurance protects you in a crisis. Even if you can't remember the last time you went to a doctor, you can't predict when you might need one in the future, making health insurance essential.

While your medical needs may be unpredictable, the cost of medical care isn't: It's just plain expensive. A trip to the emergency room or an unexpected sports injury can easily set you back more than $1,000. And a real crisis, like a serious car accident or, heaven forbid, cancer, can quickly generate tens of thousands of dollars in medical bills. In fact, medical-related debts are one of the top reasons why people file for bankruptcy protection.

One quirk of our health-care system is you'll pay far more for care if you're uninsured than if you're insured—and that's not just because insurance picks up part of the tab. Because insurers bring large numbers of patients to hospitals, doctors, and imaging centers, they also can negotiate lower rates for services.

For instance, an orthopedic surgeon may bill $3,600 for simple arthroscopic surgery. If you're uninsured, that's what you will pay. But if you have health insurance, your insurance company may have an agreement with the doctor to pay a negotiated rate of just $800. Depending on your plan, the insurance company may pay it, you may pay it, or the two of you may split it—but the cost of the procedure is still considerably less than the uninsured price.

If you're going to take risks with your finances, health insurance isn't the place to do so. Even if you work part time or aren't entitled to benefits, you need to make health insurance a priority.

DIRECTIONS

Forget trying to sort out whether you want an HMO (Health Maintenance Organization), PPO (Preferred Provider Organization), or some other plan with an oddball acronym that makes no real sense. Here are the guts of health insurance: The cheapest way to go is to give up choices and flexibility in your healthcare. If you want choice and flexibility, either you will pay largely up front, with deductions from your paycheck, and pay less when you go to the doctor or the hospital, or you pay less up front and a whole lot more when you use medical services.

There are two sets of costs in health insurance: the premium, or the amount paid for health insurance coverage, and the portion of your health expenses that you pay as you use medical services.

On average, companies pay 70 percent to 80 percent of the premiums and employees pick up the rest. That's the amount that is deducted from each paycheck.

When you consider your company's various health insurance options, start with the different costs of the different plans (usually presented on a single sheet), and then dig through the booklet with more detailed plan information to compare what each plan offers. You'll see a whole list of variations:

➤ The *deductible* is the amount you must pay in any calendar year before your basic insurance kicks in. Because insurance protects you from major problems, not minor ones, deductibles are standard with car insurance and homeowner's and renter's insurance, as well as health insurance. Will the health plan require you to pay $300, $500, $1,000, or even $2,500 before your insurance covers hospital stays, lab work, and X-rays?

➤ Some plans cover regular doctor visits from the beginning to encourage you to get medical treatment before something big happens. You often are responsible for a *copayment* to the doctor's office, usually around $20 or $25. The insurance company will pay the rest. Other plans may require you to meet your deductible before office visits are covered.

➤ Once the deductible is paid, most plans cover 70 to 90 percent of the cost of a hospital stay or an MRI. You pay the remaining amount.

➤ Many plans these days have a list, or *network,* of doctors, labs, and hospitals that have agreed to set prices. Does the plan pay a bigger percentage of the bill if you use *in-network* providers and less for those who aren't on the list?

➤ Does the plan require you to pick a *primary care physician,* who will be your main doctor? And can you schedule a visit with a specialist on your own, or does your primary doctor have to refer you to one for health insurance to cover it?

➤ Do you have dental care? Is the cost reasonable enough to make it worthwhile? And if you don't buy it, will you still see your dentist regularly for cleanings?

➤ What else is covered? Do you need to pay extra for vision care, including eye exams, glasses, or contact lenses—and is it worth it given your eye-care needs? What's the coverage on prescription medicines? Can you take advantage of a mail-order prescription service for medicine you use regularly?

➤ The *out-of-pocket maximum* is the total amount you must pay for health-care services in a calendar year before insurance will pick up 100 percent of the additional costs. That's usually a big number, often $2,000 or more per person. In other words, once you've paid that amount from your pocket in a combination of deductibles and your portion of hospital bills and other services, the insurance company will pay the rest of your bills for that year.

All of these choices can feel overwhelming—but that's better than having no choices at all.

If you are unemployed, self-employed, in school, or employed part time, you have other options. If you have been covered under your parents' insurance find out when that will end and arrange for your own insurance before it expires. You may be able to extend your coverage under your parents' policy for up to three years under a law known as COBRA, in which case you will have to notify the insurance company before your insurance lapses. You will also pay more than your parents did for your insurance, but you'll have it and you'll have time to find an alternative before COBRA runs out.

You can also buy individual health insurance, though you will pay far more for far less health insurance than your 9-to-5 peers. The good news is that more insurers are offering packages for individuals. Check the Web sites of large insurers like Aetna, Cigna, United Healthcare, Humana, WellPoint, or your local Blue Cross Blue Shield for their offerings. Or go to www. Insure.com to get quotes.

When you compare insurance options, check for any exclusions for "pre-existing conditions" or medical conditions that you already have. Depending on your state laws, companies may refuse to provide individual insurance coverage for those conditions for some period of time or they may not cover them at all. (By contrast, under federal law, group health insurance like that offered by companies cannot exclude coverage for pre-existing conditions for more than eighteen months.)

You should also investigate whether any of your professional groups, trade unions, or religious organizations offer insurance to members; group insurance may be cheaper than an individual policy. If you have difficulty finding insurance, check with your state insurance department for additional options.

If you are between jobs or schools, many of the big insurance companies offer reasonably priced short-term coverage for up to six months. Check their Web sites for details.

THE DIRECT ROUTE

Picking a plan is easier if you can sort out your medical needs first and if you are honest about how you manage your money.

It's important to spend some time on the process because once you choose a plan, you're stuck with it for a while. Most companies allow you to change plans only once a year, usually the late fall.

To sort through the various options, look at the specifics of the plans and ask yourself these questions:

➤ Do I have enough savings, or can I save enough, to cover a large deductible? If so, you can choose a higher deductible and keep more of your paycheck until you need medical care. But if coming up with $1,000 is worrisome, choose a plan with a lower deductible and pay more upfront.

➤ Am I fussy about which doctors I see? If you want total freedom of choice in your doctors and specialists and if you're willing to pay a bit more, pick a plan that gives you the option of seeing doctors both in and out of the insurer's network. If you don't mind the restriction of seeing a primary-care physician first and accepting his or her referrals from the insurer's network, you may be able to choose a less expensive plan.

➤ Do I see doctors regularly? If so, you may prefer a plan with a lower copay.

➤ Do I take prescription medicine? Then you want to look for a plan with a good prescription drug benefit.

If you have the patience, put a pencil to it: About how much will you pay a year in premiums, deductibles, and copays? These sample health insurance cost charts will give you an idea of what to expect. The USAA Education Foundation, a nonprofit organization, has a couple of worksheets to help you compare various plans, accessible from www.UsaaEdFoundation.org. These are also reprinted on the following pages. Understanding the cost of healthcare and weighing it against the restrictions and benefits will help you make the right decision for you.

MAP: SAMPLE MONTHLY PREMIUMS FOR AN EMPLOYER'S HEALTH PLAN

	Single	Employee + Spouse/Partner	Family
Health Plan 1	$25.00	$50.00	$125.00
Health Plan 2	$140.00	$280.00	$390.00
Dental Plan 1	$4.68	$18.02	$18.02
Dental Plan 2	$12.90	$45.00	$45.00
Vision Plan	$6.34	$17.18	$17.18

MAP OF THE PLANS: WHAT'S COVERED AND WHAT'S NOT

Health Plans. Plan 1 covers care only from providers in the insurer's network; those outside the network aren't covered at all. Plan 2 offers a choice, at a cost.

	Plan 1: Only in-network providers	Plan 2: Coverage for in-network providers	Plan 2: Coverage for out-of-network providers
Primary Care Physician required?	No	No	No
Deductibles	$0	$0	$300/ individual $600/family
Out of pocket maximum	$0	$1,000/ individual $2,000/family	$3,000/ individual $6,000/family
Lifetime maximum	$0	$0	$2,000,000
Doctor office visit	$10 co-pay	$10 co-pay	30% of cost after deductible is met
Specialist office visit	$20 co-pay	$20 co-pay	30% of cost after deductible is met
Preventative care/Checkups	$10 co-pay	$10 co-pay	30% of cost after deductible is met
Hospital room/ board	$0	$0	30% of cost after deductible is met
Urgent Care Center	$20 co-pay	$20 co-pay	30% of cost after deductible is met
Emergency Room visit	$125	$125	$125
Prescription drugs	$10 generic, $20 for "preferred," $40 for "non-preferred"	$10 generic, $20 for "preferred," $40 for "non-preferred"	$10 generic, $20 for "preferred," $40 for "non-preferred"

Dental Plans. Plan 1 requires that you see a participating dentist in the plan. Plan 2 allows you to see any dentist you choose.

	Plan 1	Plan 2
Deductible	None	$50 individual $150/family
Office visit	$10 co-pay	$0/deductible waived
Cleaning	$5 co-pay	$0/deductible waived
Fillings	$20–$45 co-pay	20% after deductible is met
Extraction	$20 co-pay	20% after deductible is met
Crowns	$265 co-pay plus lab cost	50% after deductible is met
Orthodontia	25% discount off specialist's fee	50% after deductible is met

Vision Plan

	Participating provider	Non-participating provider
Vision exam	$10 co-pay	Plan pays up to $50
Glasses and frames	$100 to $150 allowance	Plan pays up to $105
Contact lenses—elective	$130 allowance	$150*
Contact lenses— medically necessary	Covered in full	$300*

* Benefit takes the place of the exam, lenses, and frames

MAP: COMPARING HEALTH INSURANCE PLANS

Ask The Following General Questions:	Plan A	Plan B	Plan C
Can I choose a primary care provider (PCP) or will I be assigned to one?			
Are there a variety of PCPs to choose from in the plan?			
Can I self-refer to a specialist, or must my PCP refer me?			
Is pre-authorization required before going to the hospital or for tests or procedures?			

Ask The Following General Questions:	Plan A	Plan B	Plan C
Do I have to file my own claims?			
How soon will coverage begin after the plan goes into effect?			
If applicable, will the plan treat my pre-existing condition?			
Will the plan cover me if I am traveling?			
Will the plan provide coverage for critical or long-term illness such as cancer?			
Can I choose a hospital or will one be assigned?			
Does the plan work in conjunction with a health savings account?			
Check All Included Covered Services:	Plan A	Plan B	Plan C
Office visits			
Physical exams, health screenings and preventive care			
Prenatal and maternity care			
Immunizations			
Cancer screening tests (mammograms, pap smears, colorectal and prostate cancer tests)			
Cholesterol screening			
Laboratory tests and X-rays			
CAT scans, MRIs and other diagnostic tests			
Prescription medications			
Vision care, eye exams and eyeglasses or contacts			
Dental exams, braces and cleaning			
Mental health services and counseling			
Hearing exams and hearing aids			
Home health care			
Rehabilitation facility care			
Home medical equipment			
Physical therapy			
Speech therapy			
Adult day care			
Nursing home care			
Hospice care			

Check All Included Covered Services:	Plan A	Plan B	Plan C
Drug and alcohol abuse treatment			
Alternative treatments (acupuncture, chiropractic, etc.)			
Experimental treatments			
Outpatient surgery			
Check All Included Covered Hospital Services:	Plan A	Plan B	Plan C
Emergency care			
Ambulance services			
Physician visits			
Transplant surgery			

Materials provided by the USAA Educational Foundation, a nonprofit organization, copyright ©
2008 by The USAA Educational Foundation. See also www.usaaedfoundation.org.

Map: Comparing Health Insurance Plans Costs

Use this work sheet to compare the costs of health insurance plans.	Plan A	Plan B	Plan C
1. What is the annual deductible?			
For an individual			
For a family			
2. What is the annual premium?			
For an individual			
For individual and spouse			
For individual and family			
For a family			
3. What is your co-payment each time you use a service? (To estimate your annual cost, multiply the co-payment by the number of times you expect to use the service during the plan year.)			
Physician visit co-payment			
Hospital visit co-payment			
Prescription co-payment			
Other services co-payment			
4. What is the maximum amount you may pay out-of-pocket in each year or a lifetime?			
5. What percentage of the cost will you be responsible for after you reach your deductible?			

Use this work sheet to compare the costs of health insurance plans.	Plan A	Plan B	Plan C
6. What will you pay if you use providers outside the health plan's network?			
7. How much will services not covered by the plan cost you annually?			
8. Are there limits on days or services covered or the amount the plan will pay each year?			
9. What is the limit on what the plan will pay for a major illness?			
10. What is the limit on what the plan will pay over your lifetime?			

Materials provided by the USAA Educational Foundation, a nonprofit organization, copyright © 2008 by The USAA Educational Foundation. See also www.usaaedfoundation.org.

OTHER DIRECTIONS

When you choose your plan in the late fall, you may also be able to sign up for a flexible spending account or a health savings account. While they sound alike—and both allow you to set aside money before taxes—they are quite different.

Flexible spending accounts allow you to use pretax money to cover the health-care costs that come out of your pocket. Every fall, you have to decide how much to put away for the coming calendar year.

Since the account saves you on taxes, it's worth trying to use it. But one very significant distinction of a flexible spending account—and an important point to remember—is that it is finite, or only good for roughly a calendar year. If you don't use the money, you lose it. (Some companies allow a two-and-a-half-month grace period, so you may have fourteen and a half months to draw down the account.) It's better to guess too low than too high.

To figure out how much to put away, you have to estimate how much you'll spend out of your own pocket. In addition to deductibles and copays, you can use your flexible spending account to cover the cost of over-the-counter pain relievers and allergy medicines, physical therapy, flu shots, or other services that are not covered by your insurance. You'll have to save receipts and submit those expenses directly to the insurance company to get reimbursed.

To figure out how much to set aside, add up the obvious ones: your annual contact lens or eyeglass costs, your part of prescription drug costs, and some estimate of your deductible and doctor visits. If you are planning to have orthodontic work, laser eye surgery, or other surgery, you can get cost estimates from your doctor and put away money pretax to cover the cost when you actually have the work done. If you have money left over at the end of the year, consider a new pair of glasses or stocking up on over-the-counter medicines that you use regularly.

Health savings accounts help people who have only insurance with high deductibles. In 2009, if you are single and have a deductible of at least $1,150, you can contribute up to $3,000 in pretax money to this account to help you pay the deductible and other medical costs (The minimum deductible for family coverage must be $2,300 and the maximum contribution is $5,950.) Your company may also contribute money to your account.

Unlike flexible spending accounts, these accounts can earn interest and your money can stay there from year to year until you need it, just like an investment account. You can also take your health savings account with you if you change jobs.

If you are self-employed and can only afford health insurance with very high deductibles, a health savings account can take the sting out by giving you a decent tax break on your medical costs.

How do you remember the difference? FSAs are *finite,* or *finished,* around the end of each year and HSAs are for *high-*deductible plans.

Retirement, Already?

When there's free money, take it.

MAP IT

Admittedly, it is a little bizarre to think about retirement when it's so many years away. But if your company is like most today, its main retirement plan is a 401(k) or something similar, which requires you to make regular contributions starting now if you want to live comfortably in your old age.

To sweeten the pot, many company plans also offer some matching money from your employer, which is as close to free money as you are likely to get. Many companies will match every dollar you contribute up to 3 percent of your pay or they will match 50¢ on every dollar you contribute up to 6 percent of your pay. If you're really lucky, your employer will match even more.

Even better, the contributions you make to a regular 401(k) are pretax. (That's where the funny name comes from, section 401, paragraph k, of the federal tax code, which allows you to make your contributions before taxes.) So you'll cut your tax bill while saving for your retirement and getting extra money from your employer.

The real pot of gold is at the end of the rainbow, when you retire. Then, even a small sum invested today could be worth a boatload of money because it has had all those years to grow and compound. You won't pay taxes on a regular 401(k) until you withdraw it in retirement.

If you don't have a retirement plan at work, see "Retirement and the Tax Man" on page 255 for ways to ensure you'll have retirement options later.

DIRECTIONS

Some companies may allow you to start contributing the day you're hired, and others may require you to wait several months or even years to be in the 401(k).

Once you're eligible, it's usually up to you to sign up. However, more and more companies are automatically enrolling employees and automatically increasing the contributions they make each year.

In a 401(k) account, your money grows tax-deferred, which allows it to compound faster than regular savings. Money invested in your twenties has at least four decades to blossom before your retirement, allowing it to truly multiply.

Remember the rule of 72 from page 20? If you average an 8 percent return, your money will double every nine years. That means just $1,000 invested in your early twenties could easily be $32,000 by your late sixties. And over your career, you'll be investing much more than $1,000. The amount won't grow steadily, however. Investments tend to climb in spurts—and they can drop quickly as they did in 2008. That's why you need to invest over a long time.

While the money in a 401(k) is yours, you can't use it to pay the bills. You won't be able to get to your 401(k) funds without paying a hefty tax penalty until you reach at least age fifty-five, but more commonly fifty-nine and a half. And anytime you make a withdrawal, you will pay taxes on it, just as you would on income.

Any money your company contributes as a match may be all yours from the start, or it may "vest"—or become yours—gradually over a period of several years.

Some companies are also offering a new option, the Roth 401(k), which reverses the tax breaks. In other words, you make contributions to a Roth 401(k) after you've paid taxes. Your money grows and compounds tax free. And when you take it out at retirement, you won't owe any taxes at all on it. That means you could have much more money at retirement because you'll get to keep it all. Like the regular 401(k), however, you won't have unfettered access to your money until retirement.

The Roth 401(k) makes sense especially for people who think their tax rate in retirement may be higher than their tax rate now—which could make it an attractive choice to many young people just starting out.

Whether you enroll in a regular 401(k) or the Roth version, you will have to choose how to invest your contributions. Your plan will have a list of possible investments including mutual funds and sometimes other options, which can quickly become overwhelming.

THE DIRECT ROUTE

If at all possible, sign up to contribute enough to get your employer's maximum match. If you can't afford that much, start by contributing as much as you can, say, 1 percent to 2 percent of your pay and then increasing it as you get raises.

Contributing to a 401(k) or other plan may not be as practical if you're paying off large student loans or you have a significant amount of other debt. Some advisers will tell you to pay off all your debts first—but then you'll miss out on the long-term compounding. If you ever want to get ahead financially, saving is the only way to do it—and even a 1 percent contribution is a start. In addition, you will learn to live on less than every dollar you make, a skill that will pay off in retirement when you won't need as much in savings to continue to live comfortably.

If you make a lot of money, aim to contribute the maximum amount allowed to a 401(k), $16,500 in 2009. In addition to building your retirement fund more quickly, you'll appreciate the tax savings.

Picking between a regular 401(k) and a Roth, if your company gives you a choice, can be confusing. For a young person, the Roth version can be particularly lucrative in the future—but less so today. Because the Roth contribution is after tax, your $100 contribution to the Roth version will result in a smaller paycheck than the same pretax contribution to a regular 401(k).

So here's a suggestion: Aim to contribute enough to a regular 401(k) to get your company's match. Free money is just too precious to pass up. If you can contribute more than what your company matches and you have both options, then weigh your preferences: Do you want to give up the tax break today for one later? If so, contribute an additional amount to the Roth 401(k) because there's a good chance that your tax rate forty years from now will be higher than today, and the Roth 401(k) could put you way ahead.

But if you need every penny of your paycheck now, stick with the tax break and the regular 401(k) and you'll do just fine. Any money you put away today that can grow without being taxed puts you ahead of the game.

Some employers may make their company match to your 401(k) contribution in the form of company stock. If you have a choice, take another option. Especially in a small portfolio, you want a mix of investments, and holding just one stock, even a good one, won't give you that diversity.

Once you've settled on your contributions, you have to decide how to invest them. Picking your investments can be scary and frustrating. Many 401(k) plans now offer *target*, or *life-cycle*, funds, which take the guesswork out by allowing you to invest your money in one diversified fund and forget about it. A twenty-five-year-old in 2009, for instance, might pick a 2050 target-date fund. This is a perfectly good option, especially if you don't have the time and inclination to research the other funds.

For other ideas about how to invest your money, see "Beginning to Invest" (page 219) and other chapters in the investing section. Your employer may also recommend different mixes of funds for different age groups and investors' willingness to take more or less risk.

One other important decision is worth noting: When you set up a 401(k), you must designate a *beneficiary,* who will inherit the money if you were to die. This may seem morbid or silly, but it's an extremely important decision. Retirement funds and life insurance are distributed based on the beneficiary form, not on your will or other directions. So the money will go to your spouse or the person on this form no matter what your will says. For guidance about designating a beneficiary, see "Other Benefits," page 100.

WRONG TURNS

When you leave a job, that little pile of 401(k) savings you've accumulated can look awfully tempting, even after you pay taxes and the 10 percent early-withdrawal penalty. After all, there might be a new car or house down payment in there.

Don't do it.

The money you invest first is the most valuable because it has the longest to grow. It could become a substantial amount by the time you retire. Cashing it out now could set you back further in the long term than you realize.

If you have more than $5,000 in a plan, you can leave it where it is after you leave the employer if you like the investment options. If you'd prefer other investment choices, you can roll the money directly into an Individual Retirement Account or into a 401(k) at your next employer. A brokerage or mutual-fund firm or your plan administrator at your current employer can help you with the paperwork. But take your time; there's no deadline for making these kinds of moves.

OTHER DIRECTIONS

For retirement calculators and other worksheets, try www.Bankrate.com or Wps.fidelity.com/401k/tools.htm.

Stock Options and Stock Purchase Plans

Investing in your company,
and maybe building wealth, too.

MAP IT

Generally, stock options are perks given to top managers. But many tech companies and a smattering of other companies, like Starbucks, grant stock options each year to the rank-and-file, allowing more employees to experience shareholding firsthand.

In addition, many companies with publicly traded stocks allow employees to buy company shares at a discount, sometimes once a year and sometimes more often than that, depending on the stock purchase plan.

If your company is healthy and growing and the stock is a good one, investing in it could be an effective way to build some wealth.

DIRECTIONS

A stock option is an opportunity to buy stock in the future at a set price. Companies often award them as a supplement to other compensation, though there is no guarantee that options will have any actual value.

For instance, say you receive seventy-five options to buy shares of Your Company Inc. at $20 a share, vesting over three years. That means you are eligible to buy twenty-five shares next year at $20 a share, a total of fifty shares in two years, and all seventy-five shares in three years. If the price of Your Company stock is higher than $20, you'll make a profit. If the price is lower than $20, you won't bother to exercise your options because they are *under water*, or below the exercise, or *strike*, price.

Typically, you'll have seven to ten years to exercise your options before the offer expires. If you leave Your Company, you may lose the options you've accumulated.

Usually, companies deposit your options with a brokerage firm so when you are ready to exercise them and sell, you call the firm and give it your instructions. Options are usually exercised at the strike price and then sold at the current price. In other words, if the price of Your Company climbed to $40 and you were ready to cash in, you would exercise all seventy-five shares at $20 a share, costing $1,500. The brokerage firm would then sell the shares for $3,000, giving you a $1,500 profit before taxes. (Your actual profit will be less after taxes.)

Employee Stock Purchase Plans are a different animal altogether. They typically allow you to buy your company's stock at a 15 percent discount, based on the price on a specific day. You can buy the stock with your own cash during the purchase period or choose to have a percentage of your paycheck automatically deducted for stock purchases.

If you choose a deduction from your paycheck, some companies will give you the lowest price for the stock at either the beginning or end of the purchase period. Here's how it works: Assume a company sets the purchase price based on its stock's closing price of, say, $50 on July 1, the beginning of the purchase period. Then, if the stock price is, say, $45 on July 1 of the following year, you'll get your 15 percent discount off the $45 price; the extra money from your paycheck deductions will be refunded to you.

THE DIRECT ROUTE

Investing in your company's stock at a discount can be a real boon if the company's business is solid and well run. But any real gains will take time, and you'll want to be sure in the meantime that your investments are diversified and you don't have too much of your money tied up in one stock. Unless you're a company founder, you never want any single investment to be more than 20 percent or 25 percent of your total savings.

In the grand scheme of things, buying your company's stock at a discount through a stock-purchase plan should come after paying off your credit cards, reducing any other expensive debt, building an emergency fund, paying for health insurance, and contributing to a retirement account. If you've done all that and can afford it, go for it. You could benefit long term from the stock purchase.

Some companies even allow you to buy their stock at 85 percent of the price and then turn around and sell it a few days later, just about guaranteeing a profit. That's not a terrible strategy, but most stocks worth owning are worth owning for years, not for days. If you flip the stock, you'll pay federal taxes on your gains as if they were regular income.

By contrast, if you own your company's stock for at least a year, the investment will be considered long term, meaning that when you sell it, you'll pay federal taxes on your profit at the lower long-term capital gains rate, currently a maximum of 15 percent.

Stock options, too, can provide a bonanza if the company's stock price climbs above your strike price. However, depending on how the options are structured, you may pay taxes on any profits as if they were regular income.

You'll need to keep the important dates in mind, like when the options have vested and when they expire. You'll also need to keep an eye on the stock price. When you have a comfortable profit in your options, seriously consider selling them. Catching a peak in a stock price is difficult and if you wait too long for a higher price, the stock could slide and you could lose your opportunity to benefit from the options.

Other Benefits

There may be lots of goodies in the fine print.

MAP IT

Behind the endless paperwork of a new job might be a few extras that will save you money, make your life a little easier, or help you look like a big shot. They're worth checking out.

In addition, sometimes you can negotiate for better benefits or other perks when you can't get a better salary.

DIRECTIONS

Beyond health insurance and retirement plans, most companies offer other benefits. Among the most common are these:

➤ Paid holidays and vacations. Before you start work, you'll want to know when you qualify for time off and how much you get each year, especially if your mom is nagging you to visit.

➤ Sick leave. You may be entitled to a few days of pay when you are sick. Some companies let you accumulate and keep days for later if you don't use them this year. Other companies may combine holidays, vacations, and sick days into one overall allotment of paid time off.

➤ Life insurance. This often takes the form of a flat sum or a multiple of your annual earnings. Companies may also offer employees the chance to buy additional life insurance.

➤ Disability insurance. This provides income if you are unable to work for a short or long period of time.

You may also find a range of other options:

➤ Subsidies or reimbursements for fitness expenses, which can put money back in your pocket

➤ Reimbursement for tuition, which can help you continue your education

➤ Parking subsidies or discounts on public transportation

➤ Matching contributions to colleges and universities, private high schools, and, sometimes, charities. These matches double your contribution, which can make you seem like a generous big spender and help causes you care about.

➤ Donations to agencies where you volunteer, based on the hours you volunteer

➤ Help with child care

➤ Pet insurance

THE DIRECT ROUTE

It depends on the company and the circumstances, of course, but vacation time is often negotiable when you start a new job. If you aren't ecstatic about your pay or other benefits, that's one perk you may be able to improve. You may also be able to negotiate help with parking or public transportation.

If you have to pay for disability insurance in order to have it, it's worth considering, especially if it's relatively cheap. Disability insurance pays a portion of your paycheck if you cannot work for a period of time. Under those circumstances, you might be eligible for Social Security, but it wouldn't pay very much and it can take years to qualify. Disability insurance might help provide a livable income in a crisis, and you will be very glad you have it if you ever need it.

On the other hand, life insurance isn't really necessary unless you have a spouse or children. If you are young and single, you probably don't need to pay extra for life insurance coverage (see "Life Insurance," page 262).

If you have life insurance as part of your pay package or if you have a 401(k) or Individual Retirement Account, or all three, you need to designate a beneficiary for each one. That's the person who will receive the insurance or inherit the 401(k) or IRA in the event that you pass away.

As mentioned earlier, the beneficiary you designate will get the life insurance proceeds or your 401(k) money regardless of what your will might say, so choose carefully and keep the form up to date. You should take a look at it every few years and when you have a major life change, such as a marriage or divorce.

If you want to leave your insurance or retirement savings to someone who is younger than eighteen, you'll also need to designate a *custodian* or *trustee* until the youngster turns eighteen. Leaving it to a minor without an adult guardian or trustee can cause all kinds of legal complications.

PAYING TAXES

Maybe the least fun you'll have all year.

MAP IT

No one *wants* to do it. But just about all of us have to pay income taxes by April 15 of each year.

The forms and related instructions look intimidating. After all, the tax packets that come in the mail can be more than a hundred pages. But truly, the instructions aren't that difficult. Many single people can use the simplest form, the 1040EZ or the next step up, the 1040A. Unless you're self-employed, taxes don't get really complicated until you own real estate.

If you keep decent records and hang on to the W-2 that your employer sends you and the 1099s that your banks and others may send you, filling out tax forms should be tolerable. The real pain is in seeing how much tax you pay each year.

DIRECTIONS

Like health insurance and retirement plans, you need a special vocabulary to decipher taxes.

Let's start at the top, with *income*. How much money came in last year?

The IRS will ask you to add up all the taxable money that came in—your wages, bonuses, tips, interest earnings, dividends, and gains from selling stocks and other investments. That's your *gross income.*

This is where those pretax items on your paycheck come in handy. If you saved for retirement in a 401(k) or put money in a flexible spending account, those dollars won't be included in your gross income.

If you had a job during the year, your employer will report your wages and tips on a W-2 form, which must be sent to you by January 31 of the next year. You will attach that form to your tax return if you file by mail, and the numbers on it have to match the numbers you report to the IRS.

Next, tax laws give you several ways to adjust your income downward. If you contributed to an Individual Retirement Account, paid your own tuition, moved for a new job that was at least fifty miles away, or paid up to $2,500 in interest on student loans, you may be able to reduce your income, depending on how much you made and on tax laws, which can change from year to year. This subtotal is your *adjusted gross income.*

You also get two other nice breaks: an exemption for yourself, your spouse, and any dependents and a standard deduction. If you were single in 2009, you would get a $3,650 exemption and a standard deduction of $5,700, knocking a total of $9,350 off your gross income. Say you made $40,000 and could subtract $1,000 in student-loan interest. After subtracting your exemption and standard deduction, your *taxable* income would be $29,650.

About a third of taxpayers *itemize,* or list, their deductions for a bigger tax break rather than taking the standard one. You would do that only if your total deductions exceed your standard deduction. Deductions include mortgage interest, state and local taxes, property taxes, charitable contributions, and large medical costs, among others. Even though itemizing is more complicated and requires the dreadful 1040 form and

Schedule A, you should tackle it if it's appropriate for you. You're entitled to the tax savings that could result.

Your taxes are calculated based on your taxable income, based on graduated rates. If you are single in 2009, you will pay the following:

- ➤ 10 percent tax on taxable income up to $8,350
- ➤ 15 percent tax on taxable income between $8,350 and $33,950
- ➤ 25 percent tax on taxable income between $33,950 and $82,250
- ➤ 28 percent tax on taxable income between $82,250 and $171,550
- ➤ 33 percent tax on taxable income between $171,550 and $372,950
- ➤ and 35 percent tax on taxable income over $372,950

Map: Tax Brackets

So if your taxable income was $29,650, you would pay about $4,030 in taxes.

Last, you may also qualify for education credits or other credits that reduce your actual taxes, so check the list on the 1040 to see if any apply.

The final step is comparing the taxes you owe to the amount that your employer withheld from your check. If the withholding is more than your taxes, you'll get a refund. If not, you'll send money to the IRS.

Tax laws are constantly changing, so check with a tax professional or the Internal Revenue Service for the latest information. The IRS has a helpful Web site at www.IRS.gov.

THE DIRECT ROUTE

Filling out tax forms on your own isn't that difficult if your income is straightforward—but you don't have to do it. Online and store-bought tax software is so simple and sophisticated that it has made tax preparation relatively easy. You don't even have to pick which form to use.

TurboTax (www.Turbotax.intuit.com), TaxCut (www.Taxcut.com), and TaxACT (www.Taxact.com) are among the best known tax packages. If your adjusted gross income was $56,000 or less in 2008, you could also file your return with the IRS for free using the FreeFile service. (Go to www.IRS.gov and click on the FreeFile link on the left.) The FreeFile service will direct you to a number of online software providers that can help with your return and help you file.

You can even pay online if you owe money or sign up to have your refund directly deposited in your bank account.

If you want to fill in your own forms, first figure out the easiest tax-return form you can use. If you simply had wages and a little bit of bank interest, you can probably use Form 1040EZ, which lumps together your exemption and standard deduction into one simple subtraction problem. Use Form 1040A if you paid student-loan interest, had dividend income, or contributed to an Individual Retirement Account.

If you are self-employed, sold stock, want to claim moving expenses, or plan to itemize your deductions, you'll need Form 1040.

If you mail your return, don't forget to sign and date it. Consider sending it by certified mail to be sure it gets there.

You can also hire a tax preparer for a fee, but keep in mind that you are ultimately responsible for the accuracy of your filing. The IRS also will help taxpayers on the phone, by e-mail, or in person at local assistance offices.

Whatever you do, don't procrastinate. Paying late will cost you in steep penalties and interest. If you are due a refund, the sooner you get your forms in, the sooner you'll get your money.

PART III

SPENDING IT:
THE BIG STUFF

Every once in a while, you make a really big financial decision, the kind that sets your path for the foreseeable future. It could involve taking on substantial debt for several years. It might be an ongoing commitment for monthly rent. But in making that decision, you determine not just the size of your bank account and your spending money, but your lifestyle now and maybe for years to come.

These financial crossroads can make all the difference in how you see and present yourself, and in your day-to-day life. Will you go into debt for the fancy new car or stay with the clunker you have for a couple more years? Will you stretch for a bigger house or a nicer neighborhood or will you choose a bungalow that fits well within your budget? Can you handle a roommate for a few more years or do you need to pony up for a place of your own? And what other changes will you have to make if you go one way or another?

Ultimately these are difficult decisions because they affect your well-being and personal satisfaction as well as your finances. This section tries to help with guidelines for sorting out the tough questions and balancing your big ideas and your bank account, starting with a section on negotiating, a crucial skill when you make big-ticket purchases.

❦

NEGOTIATING

To get what you want, you'll have to ask.

MAP IT

You've been negotiating your whole life: Whenever you argued with your parents for a later curfew, tried to change a deadline with a teacher or boss, or even attempted to talk your way out of a speeding ticket, you were negotiating. But somehow, the process can seem unsavory when it involves strangers and money.

Get over it. This is your money and you're entitled to get a good deal when you buy things—especially pricey ones. You'll almost certainly have to wrangle over the price you pay for a car or a home. But you can also save money or fees if you are willing to negotiate your rent or cell phone, the prices of furniture and electronics and even medical bills and fine art. Especially in times when the economy is weak, buyers have the upper hand and can save big money through savvy negotiations.

Keep your eye on your goal and stay positive. If you don't get exactly the price you want, you still can choose whether to buy or walk away.

DIRECTIONS

The first step to effective negotiation is to do your homework. Whether you're shopping for an apartment or a mattress, you'll need to know what's available in your area and comparable prices. What do other properties rent for in the same neighborhood? In similar neighborhoods? What do mattresses with the same features sell for elsewhere?

What do others with your qualifications make in similar jobs? (Ask around, or check out www.Salary.com.)

How much does that electronic item cost on various Web sites?

Once you know the financial options, you'll have to decide what you're willing to pay or accept. If you don't get the absolute best deal, is there an amount that you can live with? What extras could be thrown in to sway your decision, such as free delivery or a service plan with a major purchase or extra vacation days in the case of a job?

After figuring out what you want to pay, think about how you will pay for purchases. Will you need to transfer money into your checking account or increase the credit limit on your credit card? Can you be preapproved for a car loan or home mortgage? The more prepared you are to make the purchase, the more attractive you will be as a buyer, and the more leverage you'll have in landing a better deal.

When you're ready to shop, take your research with you, along with questions for the sellers. Plan to take notes. That will help you remember facts and figures later, and you may hear details that will give you an edge in negotiations. Are the salespeople pushing certain models? Are they eager to move one kind of product over another? Will they match or beat competitors' prices?

Think about presenting your case in the most positive light. Because you can't know exactly what those on the other side of the table are thinking, look for ways your request might benefit them. What does the boss get from you if you are hired or promoted? Why is your offer one that the other side should take? Emphasize, for instance, why you are a low risk for a loan or that you are prepared to make a purchase right away.

THE DIRECT ROUTE

Negotiation experts say that talking face-to-face is often the most effective way to make your case. There are exceptions, however. For example, e-mail has made car negotiations quicker and less painful. Still, once you get close to a deal, you may want to close it and tie up the final details in person.

Many negotiations end with both sides relatively satisfied—and that's a good thing. There doesn't have to be a winner and a loser. In fact, it's easier to do business again later if both of you feel like a deal was fair.

Consider the alternatives if you reach an impasse. Even if the deal isn't what you want, is it good enough for you to accept? Are there other options, or are you better off reaching a less-than-perfect agreement?

If you're negotiating a price, you can start with a number below what you hope to pay to give you room to move, or you can make your best offer and stick with it. Either way, make an offer that isn't a round number—like $14,358 for a car. Silly? Yes, a little—but it will look like you really did your research and came up with your number for good, solid reasons.

Be persistent—without being rude—and consider "no" a possible starting point. Ask why the answer is negative and whether there is another way or approach that you aren't considering. What you learn could help you get the deal you really want and be an even better negotiator in the future.

Taking Out Student Loans

Paying for college can be challenging,
but there are options to ease the burden.

MAP IT

As the costs of tuition, room, and board grow exponentially, paying for college can be more daunting than ever. Ultimately, though, a college education is worth it. This is one purchase that clearly pays off long term in the form of more job opportunities and higher pay.

Because of that, borrowing is a reasonable and acceptable option. But as with any debt, you should proceed with caution, first figuring out what you (and, if you're lucky, your parents) can realistically pay, both from savings and ongoing earnings. Are there other relatives who will help or who might make interest-free loans? In addition to what a college or university might offer you in grants, are there other scholarships you can apply for to help reduce the load?

The less you have to borrow—and thus, the less you have to repay—the better off you will be both right after you graduate and for years down the road.

DIRECTIONS

As with any debt, the lower the interest rate, the better. To get the lowest interest rates on student and parent loans, you and your parents have to start with a wickedly complicated form called the Free Application for Federal Student Aid, or FAFSA. You should fill this out even if you don't think you'll qualify for much financial aid. (And note that it's *free;* you shouldn't have to pay anyone to assist you.) There are government loans available to all students—yes, even Bill Gates' kids—but only if they have filled out the FAFSA form.

The form, available at www.Fafsa.ed.gov, requires you and your family to share all kinds of information about earnings, savings, and big expenses to see if you qualify for certain kinds of aid. To complete it, you'll need tax returns, bank statements, and investment records. You'll also need to file it early in the calendar year. For instance, if you are looking to borrow for the 2009–10 school year, you should file the form in the first half of 2009—the earlier, the better—using tax-return information from 2008. You can even file as early as January 1 using preliminary numbers that you can revise later.

To actually receive financial aid, including some loans, you'll probably also need to apply for financial aid at the colleges you hope to attend. Individual schools may have different forms and requirements and different kinds of scholarships and loans available in addition to federal loans and grants.

Several wealthy schools have changed their requirements recently to increase grants and scholarships and to reduce or eliminate the debt their students must take on. If you are going to need financial help, you should get familiar with a school's financial aid policies before you apply.

Government aid is paid to your school's financial aid office, where it is applied first to tuition, room, and board. Anything left over is turned over to you for other expenses.

There is a kind of hierarchy of aid. Seek it out in this order:

➤ Need-based grants and scholarships. These are one of the hardest kinds of aid to get. Like gifts, they do not have to be repaid. The federal government and individual states have some grant money such as Pell Grants, many universities have their own grant and scholarship money, and organizations like community groups and advocacy groups may give scholarships to those who have financial need. To find a potential fit for you, try www.FastWeb.com, the Pay for College section at www.CollegeBoard.com, www.CollegeAnswer.com, or sites from other recognized names. Beware of scams: You should never have to pay or give a credit card number to get a scholarship.

➤ Merit scholarships. If you have good grades and board scores, you may qualify for university scholarships regardless of your family's needs. Check university Web sites to see what kinds of merit scholarships they award. You'll have a better shot at schools where your grades and test scores are above the average of admitted students'.

➤ Perkins loans. These federal loans are awarded by a school's financial aid office to students with significant financial need. Undergraduate students can borrow up to $4,000 per year at a 5 percent annual interest rate. The government pays the interest while the students are in school and for nine months after leaving school. Students then have ten years to repay the debt.

➤ Stafford loans. These government loans, the largest source of loans for college, are particularly attractive because they offer money at interest rates well below the going rate for private loans. In addition, the loans have several repayment options, and you can defer your payments for a time, if necessary.

For students who have a demonstrated need, the annual interest rate was 6 percent in 2008–09 and will fall to 5.6 percent in 2009–10. The rate is scheduled to decline for two more years. The government will pay the interest during college for these students.

MAP: INTEREST RATES ON STAFFORD LOANS FOR STUDENTS WITH FINANCIAL NEED

Loan made on or after	And made before	Interest rate
July 1, 2008	July 1, 2009	6.0 percent
July 1, 2009	July 1, 2010	5.6 percent
July 1, 2010	July 1, 2011	4.5 percent
July 1, 2011	July 1, 2012	3.4 percent

➤ Other students are still eligible for Stafford loans, but pay 6.8 percent interest and can defer the interest payments while in school, adding them to the loan for repayment when they're done.

➤ Repayment of these ten-year loans starts six months after school is done. Stafford loans come with origination and default fees, which are deducted from the loan amount.

➤ Freshmen can currently borrow up to $3,500 in Stafford loans; sophomores can borrow up to $4,500; and juniors and seniors can borrow $5,500 a year, with some exceptions.

➤ PLUS loans. These are ten-year government-backed loans for parents that carry a fixed interest rate of 8.5 percent. They also come with fees, and interest and principal payments start about sixty days after the loan is finalized. The limit on how much can be borrowed depends on the parents' ability to pay.

➤ Home-equity loans. Some parents may find it cheaper to borrow against the equity, or ownership, they have built up in their homes than to simply borrow directly from a bank. Interest on these loans may be tax deductible.

> ➤ Private loans. Many banks will make their own education loans to students and parents without government backing. Interest rates are based on credit scores, but are always higher than the government loans, meaning you will pay much more over the life of the loan. Because they are so expensive, these should be the loans of last resort.

THE DIRECT ROUTE

Wading through financial aid forms and filling out loan applications is no picnic. But the payoff for paying attention and doing the legwork can be big. Students who borrow for college take on an average debt of more than $20,000 and will pay $8,000 or more in interest over the ten-year life of their loans. Your goal should be to keep your debt load to loans that are absolutely necessary.

If you need help with the forms and understanding the process, talk with a guidance counselor, contact a college financial aid office, or call the help lines listed on the FAFSA Web site. You shouldn't have to pay someone to help you navigate the aid process.

If the financial aid offer from a particular school seems unworkable, you should talk with the financial aid office. Some packages may be negotiable. Some schools will match packages from other schools and most will consider other issues, like medical expenses, siblings in college, one-time payments that may distort income, or other extenuating factors.

You have to reapply for financial aid every year, and schools are likely to expect you to borrow proportionately more each time. Because of federal loan limits, you can't borrow as much as a freshman as you can as a senior. So financial aid offices may cut grants and increase the loan portion of your package as you go through school. You can try to negotiate changes, especially if your family circumstances have changed.

To keep your total borrowing in check, try to estimate your first-year salary after you graduate and make that the maximum total amount that you borrow. If you can keep your first-year loan payments to a maximum of 10 percent of your first-year pay, you should be able to comfortably repay your loans in ten years. Borrow more than that, though, and you may be still paying off your loans when your children go to college.

Government-backed loans may be awarded by the financial aid office, but you can still shop around. Most of the loans are made by banks and other private lenders, with the federal government guaranteeing lenders repayment of most of the loan. Some lenders offer incentives, such as interest-rate discounts for signing up for an automatic debit from your checking account, or other discounts if you make a certain number of payments on time. Some schools participate in a program through which you instead borrow directly from the federal government.

Varying incentives from different lenders can be hard to compare, so look specifically for discounts that apply sooner rather than later—you'll save more in interest. If you have to make four years of on-time payments to get a lower interest rate or reduced principal, there's a good chance you'll never see that perk. Choose loans where the upfront fees are less and discounts kick in right away.

ADDITIONAL DIRECTIONS

One of the best Web sites on this subject is the extensive www. Finaid.org, which has calculators that help you estimate your future salary, compare loans, compare financial aid packages, and navigate other complex questions. The government site www.StudentAid.ed.gov can also direct you to more information.

Repaying Student Loans

After college, be smart about your debt.

MAP IT

Paying off student loans probably isn't a top priority in the first year after college. But getting off to a smart start can make a world of difference in the years to come.

Besides, it's easy: Just pay attention to when your payments are due and make them on time.

If you can't make the scheduled payments with your current income, there are alternative ways to repay your government loans—extending their length, paying less now and more later, or structuring payments based on your income. All of these, however, carry the risk of additional long-term costs.

DIRECTIONS

As you move toward graduation, lenders may woo you to consolidate your loans. What they're asking you to do is to take all your loans and put them together into one big loan. This may make sense but it may also cost you a lot more in the long run.

If you can make your payments with your current income and if consolidating doesn't lower your interest rate, you are better off staying with the loans you have. If all your loans are with one lender, that lender will probably send you one bill each month so that you don't have to make multiple payments.

If you can lower your interest rate by consolidating your loans into one, it's worth considering. Loans issued before 2006 had variable rates that adjusted each year. Many borrowers could lower their interest rate and lock in at a fixed rate by consolidating. The option is less attractive now, however, because federal loans are offered at more reasonable fixed rates.

Keep in mind that if you consolidate, you will start over on a new loan and lose any discounts the lender initially promised you for making your payments on time.

Lenders may also strongly encourage you to consolidate your loans so that you can extend the payment time from ten years to twelve or twenty years, pointing out that the move will lower your monthly payment. But it will also greatly increase the interest you pay over the life of the loan. Switching to a twenty-year loan, for instance, will cut your monthly payment by about a third. It will also more than double the amount of interest you pay over the life of the loan.

MAP: REPAYING A $10,000 STUDENT LOAN WITH A 6.8 PERCENT INTEREST RATE

Repayment time	Monthly payment	Total paid	Total interest paid
10 years	$115.08	$13,809.66	$3,809.66
20 years	$76.33	$18,321.22	$8,321.22

The government's student-loan program also offers ways to combine your loans and pay them off based on your current income or with graduated repayment, where the initial loan payment is lower and the amount increases every two years. A new income-based repayment option begins July 1, 2009.

Both methods are intended to make the repayment process easier, but both also are likely to increase the total amount you repay.

For more information on how to qualify for the options and calculators on the impact of them, see www.LoanConsolidation.ed.gov, www.StudentAid.ed.gov, and www.Finaid.org.

THE DIRECT ROUTE

Before you leave school, write down all your loan information in one place: the lenders, their phone numbers and addresses, how much you owe, when the first payment is due, and the size of the payment. Then file that sheet in a place that you'll remember.

In addition, make sure your lenders have your e-mail address, home address, and a phone number. A shocking number of people drop the ball and miss the first payment on their student loans, getting their financial life started on the wrong foot. You want to know when your payments are due before you miss them—and mess up your credit.

If possible, take advantage of any discounts for having your monthly payment automatically debited from your checking account. Of course, you'll have to make sure you have enough money in your account each month. But it will keep you from forgetting to pay and possibly save you some dough.

If you have the cash to pay more than your monthly payment, try to actually pay off your loans early. That will free up more cash for personal savings, retirement, and actual fun stuff, like vacations. Pay off your most expensive debt first: credit cards, then private loans, followed by Stafford loans.

If you're tempted to consolidate, try to focus on the total debt and interest you will pay, not on the monthly payment. A lower monthly payment may seem tempting, but do you really want a lender to get most of the benefits of your hard work in the form of additional interest payments?

If you do consolidate, shop around for the best discounts, just as you did the first time around. You can also consolidate directly through a government program at www.Loan Consolidation.ed.gov.

If you go back to school, can't find work, join the military, or otherwise get in a financial bind, you can ask for your loans to be deferred or to pay a smaller amount for a period of time. You cannot, however, already be in default on your loans, which the government defines as failing to pay for 270 days.

Defaulting on student loans has serious consequences. Among other things, your employer could be required to hold back some of your wages, your credit record will suffer, and you could lose your tax refunds. If you fall behind on your payments, contact your lender and try to find a workable resolution before you default.

Renting an Apartment

Even a small place can be a castle.

MAP IT

There's nothing quite like having a comfortable and convenient place to come home to. Your first apartment doesn't have to be fancy or spacious, but your day-to-day life will be far more pleasant if your apartment has all the basics you need and is reasonably near your work or school.

It also helps if your place fits reasonably within your budget. Whether you rent or buy, housing will be one of your largest costs—and realistically, you aren't going to cut back on food just to have nicer digs.

Altogether, the costs of housing can be quite impressive. Finding a new home and moving in can be expensive and time-consuming in and of itself, even before you start paying monthly rent. Then, once you make the leap to living independently, you'll have other costs, including furniture and utilities, cable or satellite television, and Internet service. If you know what you're getting into ahead of time, the transition will be much smoother.

DIRECTIONS

What can you afford? That depends on how well you manage your money, what other financial commitments you have, and what kind of place you choose to rent.

Experts say you can spend up to 25 percent to 35 percent of your *total pay*—before taxes—on housing, though you'll often see 28 percent or 33 percent quoted as the magic numbers. Turned around, the landlord will want you to have monthly income that is three or four times the monthly rent.

Still, the bigger the chunk of pay that goes to rent, the tighter your budget will be, especially if you make a modest amount of money.

Consider someone making $40,000 a year. As we've already seen, federal income taxes will take about $4,250 off the top and Social Security and Medicare will take another $3,060. So, the potential renter will have roughly $32,700 in after-tax income, or roughly $2,724 a month, to pay for rent, food, clothing, health insurance and medical costs, utilities, student loans, a car, car insurance, gasoline, and some general fun.

If you spend 33 percent of your total pay on rent, as experts suggest you can, that would be $1,100 a month. That would leave about $1,600 to cover everything else. Spend more and you'll quickly be running up your credit card debt for basics.

By contrast, if you spend 25 percent of your total pay on rent, or $833 a month, you'll have another $260 a month in spending money. An even cheaper rent will give you more breathing room.

Before you head out to look at apartments, add up your obvious costs and see what you're comfortable affording. If you're in a high-cost city or you have your heart set on a certain high-dollar neighborhood, you'll probably need a roommate or two to make your finances work.

Shop around. Once you know your target figure, start to identify neighborhoods. First and foremost, you'll want an area that is safe. You may also want an apartment near grocery stores, restaurants, public transportation in big cities, and other young people. A reasonable commute to work or school is also important. If you're miles from work, you may quickly regret the choice.

The obvious way to find apartments for rent is on Craigslist or other Internet services and through ads in newspapers. In some cities, such as New York, you may have to work with a broker at a cost of as much as 15 percent of a year's rent. You should also ask friends and coworkers for ideas. Sometimes you can take over someone else's lease or sublet, meaning you rent from the person who is leasing the apartment already.

You'll want to look at a few apartments to get an idea of reasonable prices in an area. Always ask to see the apartment for rent, rather than a model. Make sure the appliances work, the locks lock, and the apartment is clean and in good shape.

Once you decide on an apartment, be prepared to pay up. You may be asked to pay an application fee so that the landlord can run a credit check on you. Depending on what part of the country you're in, you may be required to put down a security deposit of a few hundred dollars or a month or more of rent to ensure that you won't wreck the place. (You should get that back if the apartment is in good shape when you leave.)

You'll also have to pay the first month's rent and in some cities, the last month's rent as well.

You'll then be asked to sign a lease, a legally binding contract that spells out the terms of your agreement. Once again, consider it a treasure hunt and find these answers:

➤ How long will the lease last? And when it expires, will you go month-to-month or have to sign a new lease?

➤ What is the rent and when is it due? Under what circumstances can the landlord raise the rent?

➤ What utilities are covered? Do you or the landlord pay for electricity, natural gas, water, or trash collection? Is cable TV or wireless Internet included?

➤ What else is included? Appliances? Who pays for pest control? Will there be curtains or shades, a fitness room, and parking for you and your guests? How will repairs be handled? Can you paint the walls the way you want them?

➤ How do you get out of the lease? Can you move after a certain amount of notice? Can the landlord kick you out before the lease is up? If you decide to move, can you sublet the apartment to someone else until the lease is up?

THE DIRECT ROUTE

Before you fall in love with a place, visit it several times during the week and weekend—especially at night. You won't know what the environment is like unless you experience it.

While you're there, ask other tenants about their experiences. Have there been problems with safety or repairs? How has the landlord treated them? If they have beefs, they'll almost certainly share them.

Bring along a tape measure and write down the dimensions of the rooms. That way you'll know if Mom's old dresser or the sofa you're fond of will fit.

The more prepared you are, the more likely you are to land the apartment you want when you find it, even in a competitive area. Bring along a letter from your employer verifying your pay and employment status, pay stubs, recent bank statements, copies of canceled rent and utility checks, and a copy of your credit report.

If you haven't rented before, you may want to also bring letters of reference; even those from professors or a dorm resident adviser verifying that you're responsible and trustworthy may help. Still, you may be asked to have your parents cosign the lease if you don't have a credit score or have a spotty credit record.

Negotiate. Don't hesitate to try to lower the rent, or reduce or eliminate some of the deposits. If there are terms of the lease that you have problems with, raise them. You may be able to make changes.

Get everything in writing. Promises and assurances are almost impossible to prove later. If the apartment manager tells you there will be a refrigerator, make sure that it's in the lease or an addendum to it.

If you are renting with roommates, each of you should sign the lease so that one of you isn't stuck financially if a roommate flakes out. You should also work out details in advance: Who will pay utilities? How will food be divided? Who will do which chores? How will the rent be paid if one person leaves?

Since you can be financially responsible under the lease if a roommate moves out, a roommate agreement that spells out each person's responsibilities can be helpful. Some agreements also address overnight guests, smoking and drinking, kitchen clean-up, and who buys household supplies. For examples, go to www.Gwired.gwu.edu/offcampus or www.Tenant ResourceCenter.org, or search for "roommate agreements" online.

Finally, before you move in, walk through the property with the landlord to make note of any problems. Take pictures with a time stamp so you'll have proof that the problems were there before you came along. Those can help when it's time to reclaim your security deposit.

Buying a Car

Don't let your wheels slow you down.

MAP IT

In most parts of the country, a car is a necessity. You've got to have one. But the one you choose can make a huge difference in your finances and your lifestyle.

The challenge of buying your first car is to find the middle of the road—a vehicle you're happy to drive that also fits your budget and your transportation needs. Luckily, there are more good sources of information on cars than ever before, making it easy to do research that can save you time and money.

DIRECTIONS

In your mind's eye, you may dream of the coolest new cars—fast ones, stylish ones, ones with so many gizmos in the dashboard that they do everything but make you breakfast. Realistically, though, what you need are wheels that get you to and from work or school, to see your friends and family, and maybe to help you do your job.

➤ **What Do You Most Need?** The process should start with an honest assessment of what you really need a car to do, beyond impress your friends. How many passengers will you need to carry at once? Will two doors work, or do you need four? Do you need a big trunk or a hatchback—or maybe a truck for hauling stuff? Will you need all-wheel drive for bad weather? Will you be driving a lot, making fuel efficiency all the more important?

➤ **Will the Vehicle Be Safe?** At the least, any car you buy, new or used, should have good safety features, including driver and front passenger-seat airbags. Ideally, it will also have side air-bags and effective bumpers that will protect you in an accident. That's especially true if you're buying a smaller car in an area where sport-utility vehicles and trucks crowd the roads.

To assess the safety of the cars that interest you, look up the National Highway Transportation and Safety Administration's crash and rollover tests at www.SaferCar.gov.

➤ **Will It Be Reliable?** A nice car is no help if it's constantly in the shop. Nor is a car a bargain if multiple repairs drain your emergency cash reserves. *Consumer Reports* magazine and J. D. Power both rate cars based on their dependability and quality based on surveys of thousands of owners. If you don't want to subscribe to *Consumer Reports* or its Web site, you can look at the magazine or its annual book at your local library.

➤ **What Can You Pay Vs. What Are You Willing to Pay?** Car dealers (and maybe your friends and family members) will focus on the monthly payment. But you're going to pay the whole amount—and interest, if you finance the car—regardless of what you pay per month. If you buy a $28,000 car instead of a $20,000 car, what will you give up? Would that $8,000 pay off some student loans, furnish your place, or take you on several exotic vacations? On the flip side, will you love the nicer car so much that you will drive it for a few extra years, making up for the cost difference?

If you have your heart set on a nicer car than you can afford brand new or if you simply want to keep the cost down, a used car is a reasonable solution. Many used cars today come with some warranty protection, and well-made cars can last long beyond 100,000 miles. In addition to saving you money, used cars are also cheaper to insure. Taxes and registration fees may also be lower for older car models.

Whether you buy new or used, you should do a fair bit of research before you start negotiations, including a test drive. Though the car salesman may encourage you to make only a short trip around the block, you'll know more about the car if you put it through some paces. Try out a U-turn, make a quick stop, and if you can, take it on a highway.

Once you narrow down your choices, check the manufacturers' or dealers' Web sites for any incentives they are offering, like cash discounts or lower interest rates.

Then, research prices. The manufacturer's suggested retail price is also known as the sticker price, because that's what appears on the window sticker. The *invoice* price is closer to what the car dealer pays. You will pay something more than the invoice price, but knowing it will help you determine what you think is a reasonable price.

Edmunds.com and Kelley Blue Book, www.KBB.com, will also give you an estimate of what people in your zip code actually paid when they bought that specific model, so you have an idea of what discount you might get off the sticker price. Those prices include a big add-on known as the destination charge, the charge for getting the car from the factory to the dealership. *Consumer Reports* also sells pricing information.

To get started, you should call, visit, or e-mail several dealers, specifying what car you want, the colors you prefer, and the options that you are willing to pay for. If there aren't many dealers near you, check with some that are as far as an hour away.

Some dealers have adopted no-haggle policies, meaning they won't negotiate their offering price. If the price is reasonable—that is, close to what your research says that folks in your area are paying—you may find it worth your time and money to make a quick deal and get your new car on the road. If it isn't, keep shopping.

At traditional dealers, your experiences will vary, but you should be prepared to be cornered in a small room for a couple of hours while a salesman (or two) tries to convince you to pay more than you want to pay. This is the part of car buying that most people find exasperating.

As you near agreement on a price, ask about other charges, including sales tax and title and license fees. The total may exceed what you expect. Be sure you understand all the fees; some, like a *documentation* fee, are add-ons that may be negotiated away.

THE DIRECT ROUTE

Working out a fair deal on a car takes a lot of homework and an equal amount of determination and persistence. There's no promising that it will be a pleasant experience, but your effort should pay off. Here are some other suggestions:

➤ Be willing to walk away. If you go into a dealership with your heart set on leaving with a car, you're likely to be run over by the sales process. If the hard sell gets to be too intense or if it's obvious that you won't get your price, leave. Chances are that you'll get a better deal somewhere else—and you can always go back.

➤ Don't pay for extras you don't want. Dealers sometimes add sealants and coatings, or floor mats and pinstripes, and charge inflated prices. If you don't want the extras, you shouldn't spend your hard-earned cash on them—even though that may mean you have to find another car somewhere else.

➤ If you're worried about your willpower or negotiating skills, take along a friend who can help you keep focused on your goal.

➤ Hold off on financing talks until you have reached agreement on the car's price. Dealers may offer you a better financing deal—and raise the car price. You want a fair deal on the car's price *and* the financing.

➤ If a dealer offers you a choice between a rebate and 0 percent financing, run the numbers. You may do far better with the rebate. (See "Financing a Car Purchase," following.)

➤ Timing matters. Dealers are eager to make monthly sales goals, so they negotiate more at the end of the month. Buy convertibles in the winter and all-wheel-drive vehicles in the spring or summer, when there's less demand. As new models roll out, dealers also will cut better deals on the previous model. But that's only fair, since the older model will have less resale value once the new models are available.

➤ E-mail can be an effective—and less stressful—way to negotiate a price. But dealers may not offer their very best price via e-mail. To close the transaction, sit down face to face.

➤ If you go the used-car route, have a mechanic inspect the car before you buy. It's worth $100 to be sure you know what you're getting. Also find out if the car is still covered by a warranty.

➤ You can also check a used vehicle's accident and ownership history by running its vehicle identification number through CarFax. The CarFax information may be available for free if the car is advertised by dealers, or on sites like Kelley Blue

Book or www.Cars.com. Otherwise, it may be worth paying for it.

➤ Car dealers sell *certified used* cars that have been thoroughly inspected and often come with a warranty. You'll pay more for a certified used car but the peace of mind may well be worth the cost.

FINANCING
A CAR
PURCHASE

It's about the bottom line, not the monthly payment.

MAP IT

Because cars are expensive, how you manage your car purchases can have a huge impact on your future financial situation. Borrow heavily and often—or lease—and you will never get out of debt.

Start small and pay yourself instead of a lender, and you can have money for new cars as well as other goodies. Even if you can simply borrow less money for a shorter time period, you'll keep—and enjoy—more of your hard-earned dough.

DIRECTIONS

If you know you're going to be financing a car purchase, do a little advance planning first.

➤ **Check your FICO credit score.** (See "Credit Reports and Scores," page 47, and the chart on p. 50.) If your score is low, you'll pay a much higher interest rate, which could hike your payment to painful levels. In that case, work on improving your credit score before you start shopping and save for a bigger down payment.

➤ **Shop around for the best rates.** The car dealer is happy to lend to you, since it makes money from your loans as well as your purchase. But you may get a much better interest rate from a bank or credit union. Check www.Bankrate.com for rates in your area.

➤ **Put away for a down payment.** The bigger the down payment, the less you'll have to borrow.

➤ **Be realistic about your budget.** The new-car excitement wears off after a few months. If your payment is so large that you can never eat out, you may soon regret the decision.

Car loans can run from a couple of years to as long as five or six. But because a car starts to lose value as soon as it is driven off the lot, those longer loans can be truly dicey. Car loans, like home loans, are structured so that you pay more interest up front and more of the principal later. That means that in year four or five, you could end up owing more on your car than your car is worth.

When you owe more than the car is worth, then you're considered "upside down" in your loan. If the vehicle were to be totaled in an accident, you would collect only the value of the car from the insurance company. You would have to pay off the remainder of the loan from your own pocket and still come up with money for a new car.

In addition, you'll pay much more overall with a longer loan. Say you borrow $15,000 at an interest rate of 7 percent. If you borrow for four years, you'll pay $359.19 a month. If you borrow for five years, your payment will fall to just under $300 a month. Looks great, right? But over five years, you'll pay almost $600 more—$17,821 in total versus $17,241 for the four-year loan.

Many people have been lured into leasing by low monthly payments and low down payments. That's enticing, for sure, but it means that you'll *always* be making a car payment. When the lease is up in three or four years, you'll have nothing to show for it. You'll have to lease or buy another car or come up with the cash to buy the used car you've been driving. You'll be much better off in the long run building ownership in a car that you can continue to drive or at least sell or trade in yourself.

THE DIRECT ROUTE

When you shop around and find a good rate at a bank or credit union, see if the lender will preapprove you for a loan. That way, you can be a *cash buyer,* able to pay for the car without having to haggle with the dealer's financing department.

In addition, by talking to other lenders first, you'll know what kind of interest rate you qualify for and can compare that with what the dealer is offering. Some dealers may try to finance your car at a higher interest rate just to make extra profit.

Apply for the shortest loan that you can comfortably pay. If you can't pay off the car in three or four years, consider whether you're buying more car than you can truly afford.

As mentioned on page 133, if the dealer offers you a choice between a rebate that reduces the price of a car and 0 percent financing, use a calculator like the one at www.Cars.com to see how it comes out. If your interest rate will be low anyway, like 1.9 or 2.9 percent, you probably are better off taking the cash. In addition, the 0 percent offer may only apply to people with the highest FICO scores and may be available only on three-year loans.

While the dealer is selling you financing, it may also try to convince you to buy an extended warranty or other items for the car that you don't really want. Before you sign the paperwork, be sure you know exactly what you are buying.

The auto industry would love for you to buy a new car at least every four or five years. But you'll be in much better financial shape if you buy used cars or aim to drive your new car for ten years or 100,000 miles.

You can also take steps to someday pay cash for your cars. Start out by buying an inexpensive but reliable car and paying it off as quickly as you can—or graciously accepting a hand-me-down from a relative. Drive it for as long as you possibly can while you make monthly payments to yourself, keeping the money in a separate online savings account, for instance.

When you absolutely must have a new car, you should have enough saved to pay for a substantial amount of the car. You may also be able to trade in your old car, further reducing the price. Hopefully, you'll have to borrow a relatively small amount, which you can pay off in a year or two. Eventually, by making payments to yourself and earning interest on them, you should accumulate enough to buy your cars outright and avoid the high cost of auto debt altogether.

AUTO INSURANCE

Protecting your car and your pocketbook.

MAP IT

Most states now require all drivers to have a minimum amount of automobile insurance—but not for *your* benefit. The state requirements are intended mostly to protect those you might hit or injure in a car accident. Driving is risky business.

Beyond the minimum required, you also need coverage for your car, yourself, and any passengers. The various pieces make insuring a car more complex than insuring your apartment or home. That's also because your car is far more likely to get tangled up in a mess than your home or apartment is.

What you pay will depend on several factors—your age and gender, the car you drive, your driving record, where you live, and also your credit record. But even if you qualify for the lowest rates, you will pay several hundred dollars a year for the coverage.

DIRECTIONS

If your state requires you to have auto insurance, it probably requires a minimum of *liability* insurance, which pays if you injure someone else in an auto accident.

There are generally three pieces to this liability coverage: coverage for bodily injury to one person, coverage for all people injured in the accident, and coverage for property damaged. A number of states, for instance, require a minimum of $25,000 in liability coverage for injury to one person; $50,000 in coverage per accident; and $10,000 to $25,000 in coverage for property damaged in the collision.

If you manage to total someone's Mercedes and have only $10,000 in coverage, that owner can go after your personal assets to cover his or her remaining losses. Your potential liability makes driving a perilous prospect and makes carrying an appropriate amount of auto insurance all the more important.

Some states also require *personal-injury protection* insurance to cover the driver's own potential medical expenses or *medical payments* insurance to cover any injuries—yours or someone else's—related to an accident. If your health plan covers you in an accident, however, you may not need personal-injury coverage.

A number of states further require you to have insurance in case you are hit by a driver who isn't insured or who doesn't have enough insurance to pay for the damages caused.

Collision insurance covers your car from damage from any kind of accident, whether you hit the garage wall, rear-end another car, or collide with a tree. *Comprehensive* coverage applies to other disasters that can befall your car, including theft of the whole car, break-ins, hail damage, or fire.

Like all insurance, you must pay a deductible, or the first part of the expenses, on each claim, before you collect from the auto insurance company. The higher the deductible, the lower the cost of your insurance, or your *premiums,* will be.

If you lease a car or if you have a long car loan, you may also need *gap* insurance, which covers the difference between what you owe on your lease or loan and what the car is worth.

In figuring out what to charge, insurance companies assess your risk as well as your record. Young men pay more than young women, and those under twenty-five years old pay more than those over twenty-five. If you have a number of speeding tickets or a history of accidents, you will also pay more for insurance.

And if you have been convicted of driving under the influence or driving while intoxicated in the last seven years, you may not be able to buy traditional car insurance at all. Instead, you'll have to buy from a state insurance pool, where you'll pay a lot more for less coverage.

Beyond your personal record, new cars are generally more expensive to insure than old cars. The more you drive, the more you'll pay. And if you live in a high-crime area, you'll pay extra for that, too.

THE DIRECT ROUTE

Be sure you understand what your policy will specifically cover and what it will cost. Premiums often may be quoted for six months of coverage, not for a full year—so you may need to double the number to know your annual costs.

Some companies also bill for four months out of every six, instead of billing every month. If your company does that, you can eliminate ugly surprises by setting aside some money every month to cover your insurance bill.

A higher deductible can lower your total cost. But if you can't swing $1,000 up front to repair your car, then go with a lower deductible.

You may get a better deal if you use the same insurer for your home or renter's insurance as for your car insurance. But you'll want to shop around for the best rates and also consider whether the insurer has a good reputation for responding promptly and paying fairly. J. D. Power ranks auto insurers based on complaints, as do some state insurance departments.

Generally, you should carry more than the minimum liability insurance to protect yourself in the case of a terrible accident. If you can afford it, coverage of $100,000 per accident is reasonable. If you have real assets to protect, like a business or measurable savings, you should carry more to protect yourself if you are sued personally.

If you get a speeding ticket, see if taking a defensive driving course can keep it off your record—and off your insurance record. You may also be able to lower your insurance costs by taking a driver's course or making sure your car has some anti-theft protection. If you are a student who makes good grades, ask your insurance company if you qualify for a discount.

Don't be afraid to shop around every few years. You may be able to find better rates.

Buying a House

A piece of the American Dream comes with a big price tag.

MAP IT

Owning a house conjures up all kinds of upbeat images: success, security, good neighbors, and nice surroundings. But more and more, it also brings to mind big bucks. In many areas of the country, buying a home is expensive, and in some big cities—New York, Boston, Los Angeles, and San Francisco—it has become stunningly so.

The enormous price increases in the early 2000s lulled many buyers into believing that home ownership was also a surefire way to make money as prices soared up and up. But as many of those buyers learned in 2006, 2007, and 2008, home prices can also sink, sometimes sharply and quickly, and the housing market is subject to the same harsh ups and downs as other markets.

If you someday want to own a home, you should buy because it's truly where you want to live, not because you are hoping for price appreciation. Homeownership is great if you want stability, both in location and in what you pay. There's also a decent tax break, depending on the size of your mortgage and your tax rate. At the same time, homeownership is also an enormous commitment of time and money, filling weekends with chores involving lawns, paint, and gutters and requiring endless repairs and maintenance.

Finding the right first home is a complex, time-consuming, and costly process. Here's an introduction.

DIRECTIONS

Are you ready for homeownership? Before you jump in, you should be secure enough in your work that you're reasonably sure to be in the same city for the next five years or so, long enough to make all the extra expense worthwhile.

You should be comfortable with the responsibilities that go with owning and keeping up a property. And you should have amassed enough money in the bank to make a down payment, cover significant new expenses like property taxes and new furniture, and still have your emergency funds intact.

The first step is usually to figure out how much house you can afford. That means jumping into the mortgage process, which will be addressed in the next chapter. Generally, though, what you can afford is a combination of your income, your down payment, your area's property taxes, current interest rates, and your comfort level.

Some well-meaning friends and real-estate professionals will encourage you to stretch for your first house with a higher house payment, especially in high-cost areas. The thinking is that your income is likely to go up and you'll be able to more easily afford the payment in a few years.

But that's very risky, especially if the local economy turns down or life throws you some unexpected curveballs. You'll enjoy your new house more if you can comfortably afford it now, not later.

Once you have a price range in mind, you should start your shopping in the car and online. Drive around and look at neighborhoods. Do you want brand spanking new? Old and funky? Close to downtown? Deep in the suburbs? Do you need a home with lots of rooms and closets or would you rather have something smaller in a more upscale area? Do you want a yard or would you prefer a condo with little upkeep?

As you narrow your choices, you can also scope out homes for sale online, getting a feel for what's available. Every Sunday, many homes for sale are open to potential buyers, allowing you to walk through and see the place up close. Visit neighborhoods at night as well as during the day to get a good feel for the areas.

If you choose a new home development, you may deal primarily with the builder's sales force. If you've settled on a few established neighborhoods, you'll want to hire a real-estate broker. Ask friends for reliable, trustworthy brokers they know or talk to brokers who seem to know a neighborhood well. (You should see their signs all over the area.)

For many years, nearly all real-estate brokers worked for the seller, who pays their commission, or fee, from the sale proceeds. In those cases, the brokers would take buyers like you around and help draw up sales contracts—but their responsibility was to the seller. Today, there are also buyers' agents who pledge to represent the buyer's interests first. Either can represent you, but you should know where your broker's allegiance is from the first appointment.

The broker should suggest ideas, show you potential homes, and give you information about other sales in the neighborhood so that you know what a fair price is. One way to compare different houses is to look at the price per square foot of living space for recent sales and for homes currently for sale.

When you settle on a house you want, the broker should help you draw up an offer. Unless the market is very hot, you will offer something less than the asking price, and the seller will respond with a counteroffer. In a market where prices are falling, there should be more opportunities for first-time buyers to negotiate a good deal if you do your research. Even so, emotions often get involved, for both buyers and sellers. The negotiating process can be intense, and you and the seller may volley several times and still not come to an agreement.

If you can't work out a price you are comfortable with, you should walk away. (Sometimes, after a cooling-off period, the two sides will talk again and can reach a deal.)

When you do finally land the house you want at a price you're happy with, you'll write your first check, which will go into a special *escrow* account, as a sign of your intent to make the deal work.

Now the process really gets rolling. In a fairly short period of time, you'll need to line up your financing, bring in an independent inspector to thoroughly check out the house (and if there are any problems, you may choose to renegotiate with the sellers), and begin the process of moving.

Assuming everything goes smoothly, your last step is the *closing*, when all the paperwork is signed and the giant checks are written and handed over. Closing can be a bone-rattling experience. In addition to your down payment, you will bring an amount equal to 2 percent or more of the home's cost to the table for processing fees, an arcane requirement called title insurance, and mortgage-related charges. You'll also pay a prorated share of property taxes and a year of homeowner's insurance.

You will get a good-faith estimate of those fees in advance. But there are often surprises—costs or terms you either weren't aware of or didn't understand. Bring your checkbook.

Finally, though, you'll have the keys. But don't think that means the costs will stop: Utilities have to be started. Something in the house may need a repair. And you may need curtains or blinds, new furniture, a refrigerator or washing machine, and other accoutrements.

THE DIRECT ROUTE

Every step along the way, you'll need to do your homework.

Be sure your broker understands your goals and is pleasant to work with, since you'll spend a fair bit of time together.

You can ask for recent references and check them out before committing.

Before you fall in love with a house, understand the neighborhood. What kind of crime does it have? How are the schools? (Even if you don't have children, decent schools will help the resale value later.) Where's the nearest grocery, park, or library? What will your commute to work be like?

Before you buy, ask if the neighborhood requires any other fees. Condominiums have maintenance fees that can add hundreds of dollars a month to your costs. Some housing developments require that everyone pay association fees.

Don't skimp on the inspection. No house will be in perfect condition, and you'll be better off if you know more about the foundation, roof, appliances, and construction. Even buyers of new homes might benefit from a critical look by an outside inspector. If major problems turn up, you will want to ask the sellers to fix them or cut the purchase price.

Be skeptical of any good-faith estimates on closing costs or loan costs. They are just that—estimates. Assume that the real costs will be higher than you think and then hope that you'll be pleasantly surprised.

Negotiate, negotiate, negotiate. The broker's commission may be negotiable. The closing costs may be negotiable. The home price is certainly up for negotiation. This is no time to be shy and complacent. It's your life savings at stake.

ADDITIONAL DIRECTIONS

To compare the cost of renting to the cost of buying, check out the worksheet at www.WSJ.com/BookTools. For more information on homeownership, go to *The Wall Street Journal. Complete Home Owner's Guidebook.*

MORTGAGES

Sometimes, debt can be your friend.

MAP IT

Most of the time, borrowing money is a downer, a drag on your finances. That's because most of the things we might buy with debt—furniture, cars, computers—decline dramatically in value or wear out not long after the debt is repaid. In a few instances, however, when the asset can actually increase in value, debt can have almost supernatural powers.

That can be the case with mortgages, a specific kind of loan for purchasing real estate. Mortgages help you buy a home that would otherwise be too expensive to purchase. In addition, because a house can increase in value over time, a mortgage can help you build wealth.

There are no guarantees, of course, that homes will appreciate. But here's how it works: Let's say you bought a $200,000 home with cash and ten years later you sold it for $300,000. In a decade, your money would have grown by $100,000, or 50 percent.

Then, let's assume you bought that $200,000 home by putting down $50,000 in cash and taking out a $150,000, thirty-year mortgage. Every month, you pay your mortgage on time, reducing the amount you owe by about $20,000 over a decade.

After ten years, you sell the house for $300,000. With the money from the sale, you pay off your $130,000 mortgage and you have $170,000 left. You have more than tripled your original $50,000 down payment.

Cool, huh? That result is why debt is sometimes called leverage, because, like a lever, it can help you lift something that would be too heavy to pick up on your own.

But a mortgage only has that power if you can handle it comfortably. If you bite off more than you can easily chew, committing, say, half your income, you could find yourself in a world of financial woes. You could struggle to make your monthly payments, and if you got behind, you could lose your house *and* your down payment, potentially devastating your finances.

In 2007 and 2008, hundreds of thousands of homeowners were unable to pay their mortgages, sometimes because they took on too much debt to begin with and sometimes because they lost jobs or fell ill, making the mortgage burden too heavy. The repercussions rippled like dominos: The bad loans hurt banks and investors, and the explosion in foreclosed properties drove down home prices. In response, the availability of new mortgages tightened.

Even in light of the housing mess, buying a house can be a good move. But that's true only if you research and negotiate carefully, make a real down payment, and still have a financial cushion to keep making your payments once you're in the home.

DIRECTIONS

What can you afford? That's an important question—and one that only you can answer. More likely than not, it's a lower number than the one you may hear from a real-estate broker or a mortgage lender.

That's because those mortgage and real-estate brokers ask

a different question: How much can you borrow? That answer is based on a combination of current interest rates, the kind of mortgage you want, and your personal finances. It should be considered the outside limit for a mortgage, not the amount you can "afford."

As a rule of thumb, lenders think your maximum monthly payment should be no more than 28 percent of your gross monthly income, or income before taxes and other deductions.

For the sake of round numbers, let's assume that you or your family makes $100,000 a year and your gross monthly pay is $8,333. The largest monthly house payment you should have is $2,333, or 28 percent of that. That payment would include your mortgage and the monthly share of your annual property taxes and homeowner's insurance.

In addition, lenders take into consideration how much other debt you have. Your total debt—student loans, car loans, the credit-card debt that you carry, and your monthly house payment—should not exceed 36 percent of your total monthly pay. If you or your family makes $8,333 a month, your total debt shouldn't exceed $3,000 per month.

In addition to these two math problems, lenders will look at your credit score to weigh whether you are a risky customer or a safe one. They also will take into consideration your savings and other assets, since your overall financial picture may improve your ability to repay the loan.

Before you actually apply for a mortgage, you'll need to shop around and do some research. Mortgages come in varying shapes and sizes, and interest rates can vary widely from firm to firm. Fixed-rate mortgages mean your interest rate— and your monthly payment—won't change over the life of the loan. The most common fixed-rate loans are for thirty years and fifteen years. Your monthly payment will be higher with a fifteen-year loan but you will pay it off faster and you will save tens of thousands of dollars in interest over the life of the loan.

MAP: A 30-YEAR HOME MORTGAGE VS. A 15-YEAR FOR A $200,000 LOAN

	30-year mortgage	15-year mortgage
Monthly payment	$1,264.14	$1,687.71
Interest rate	6.5 percent	6 percent
Total principal paid	$200,000	$200,000
Total interest paid	$255,088.98	$103,788.45

Adjustable-rate mortgages, or ARMs, start with a relatively low interest rate and usually adjust every year, sometimes jumping up by as much as 2 percentage points. Usually, there is a cap that limits how high the interest rate can go. Still, if interest rates climb after you buy your house, you can end up paying much, much more for your monthly payment than you did the first year.

Some ARMs are fixed for five or seven years, and then become adjustable-rate mortgages. Because they start with lower interest rates than fixed-rate loans, these may make sense if you don't plan to stay in the house for more than five or seven years. But they can backfire if home prices fall and you can't sell your house when you expect to.

Many local newspapers run weekly lists of interest rates for fixed and adjustable mortgages in your area. You can also find them at www. Bankrate.com or on Yahoo! Finance.

MAP: THE IMPACT OF AN ADJUSTABLE-RATE MORTGAGE

Take out a 1-year adjustable rate mortgage for $200,000, with a starting interest rate of 5 percent

Monthly payment: $1,073.64

Year 1: Interest rates rise and your mortgage rate jumps to 7 percent

Monthly payment: $1,324.43

Year 2: Interest rates continue to rise and your mortgage rate jumps to 9 percent

Monthly payment: $1,590.81

Year 3: Interest rates rise again, and your mortgage rate jumps to its maximum level of 11 percent

Monthly payment: $1,868.78

Your real-estate broker may have a list of local mortgage companies and their offerings.

If you are a first-time buyer, you should check to see if your state has any special financing or programs for first timers. In addition, the Federal Housing Administration insures loans and may have a program that works for you. FHA loans require smaller down payments and have some favorable terms for those starting out. You can find out more at http://portal.hud.gov.

If you want a smoother home-buying process, you can ask a mortgage company for an early okay. You can "prequalify" by giving a potential lender some basic financial information. In return, you'll get an idea of the maximum amount you can borrow.

"Preapproval" is a more elaborate process. The lender will check out your credit record, employment history, and other financial information and commit to lending you money for a limited period of time, with some caveats. Being preapproved may make you a more attractive buyer and give you negotiating power because sellers can have some confidence that you can complete a sale.

Be aware that you may have to pay some up-front fees for preapproval; if so, you should be fairly certain you want to use that lender before going through the process. Otherwise, you'll pay those fees all over again to someone else when you decide to buy.

After you find your dream house, you will actually apply for the loan. You'll need bank statements, investment account statements, pay stubs, and other financial information for the loan application. It might also help to put together a *net worth statement* that lists every major investment and asset that you own and its value, as well as all of your debts.

You will also discover that the mortgage world is awash with seemingly endless fees and charges, some of which are paid up front and many that are paid when you buy the house:

➤ To reduce your interest rate and your monthly payment, you can pay *points* upfront. Each point is 1 percentage point of your loan, or $2,000 on a $200,000 loan. These so-called discount points make sense if you plan to stay in the house at least five years because it will take at least that long for the savings in your monthly payment to equal what you paid up front. Try to avoid paying so-called loan origination fees equal to a half-point or point since they are just additional fees that don't reduce your monthly payment.

➤ If you don't put down at least 20 percent of the purchase price, you will need private mortgage insurance, or PMI, which is for the lender but you pay for it. Usually, it means your interest rate will be raised by half a percentage point, say to 7 percent from 6.5 percent. When you own 20 percent or more of the home thanks to price appreciation or through mortgage payments, you can ask to stop paying for PMI.

➤ To ensure the home is worth what you're paying, the lender will have it professionally appraised. You will probably pay more than $300 for that service. If the lender believes you are paying too high a price based on recent sales prices, it may turn you down or insist that you lower the price.

➤ The lender must be sure that the property is free and clear of any legal entanglements or others' debts. For that privilege, you will pay several hundred dollars for title insurance.

➤ Other fees include credit report fees, documentation fees, application fees, flood certification, notary fees, express mail or courier charges, and copying fees.

As mentioned, the lender will provide you with a good-faith estimate of the fees—though there always seem to be some surprises. You should also get an *amortization schedule,* which breaks out how much you will pay each month on the mortgage and what will go to principal and what to interest. Like car loans, mortgage loans are structured so that you pay most of your interest up front.

That means it can take years and years to build equity, or additional ownership, in your home. On a thirty-year, $200,000 mortgage fixed at 7 percent, you will make a monthly payment of $1,330.60 (before taxes and insurance). After about twenty-two years, you will have paid off half the mortgage. The second half of your loan will be paid in the last eight years. Over the life of the loan, you will repay the $200,000 and pay another $279,018 in interest.

MAP: THE AMORTIZATION SCHEDULE
HOW A 30-YEAR MORTGAGE IS PAID OFF

Assume you took out a $200,000 mortgage at 7 percent.

	Loan balance	Principal paid	Interest paid
After 5 years	$188,263	$11,737	$68,099
After 10 years	$171,625	$28,375	$131,397
After 15 years	$148,038	$51,962	$187,547
After 20 years	$114,600	$85,400	$233,945
After 25 years	$67,198	$132,802	$266,380
After 30 years	0	$200,000	$279,018

Unless your house is very inexpensive, you will be able to take the mortgage-interest payments and property taxes as an income-tax deduction, as long as all your deductions total more than the standard deduction given to all taxpayers. That tax break reduces your cost of ownership.

THE DIRECT ROUTE

How much can you reasonably pay each month toward a house, property taxes, and home insurance? If you're paying $1,200 a month in rent now and have little left over each month, can you really scrape together $2,000 a month for a house payment?

If you think you can, do it. During the months while you're poking around various neighborhoods and considering home styles, start setting aside the difference between your rent and your potential house payment. If you feel stretched—and especially if you're cheating and dipping into that reserve every month—you should reconsider what you can actually afford.

About six months before you plan to seriously bid on homes, you should check your FICO score. (See "Credit Reports and Scores," page 47.) If your score isn't very good, you won't qualify for a very good mortgage. To get a lower rate, you'll need to start paying off your other debts and cleaning up your act. You'll want as little additional debt as possible when you take on what will likely be the largest loan of your life.

You don't need to put down 20 percent when you buy a house—but the more you put down, the better. Granted, 20 percent would be a lot of money, even on a modest house, but you should aim for a minimum of 10 percent. That may require you to save for several more years or ask for a gift from generous relatives. But you'll have some cushion if prices fall, and it's less likely that you'd be in a position where you owe more than your house is worth.

Generally speaking, fixed-rate mortgages are best when interest rates are low and when you're planning on spending years in a house.

Adjustable-rate mortgages make more sense when rates are higher and if you are going to be in a house just five years or so. Then you can roll with the risk of steeper payments. Before you agree to an adjustable-rate mortgage, however, you should run the numbers. What would the maximum payment be? And could you swing that if you couldn't refinance to a fixed rate?

Beware of loans that are geared to getting people into homes they couldn't otherwise afford. These loans may call for you to pay interest, but little or no principal, meaning you never build equity in your home. Others are structured so that the loan balance grows rather than shrinks. This phenomenon is *negative amortization* and you should avoid it like the plague.

If interest rates are moving around while you're shopping for a house, consider locking in your rate. You may not get the lowest possible rate—and there may be a fee involved as well as a deadline for sealing a sale—but interest rates can sometimes jump 1 or 2 percentage points in a short time. Guaranteeing a good rate may make a difference in the kind of house you can afford to buy.

Keep in mind that some closing costs are negotiable—but not at the closing table. Go over the costs with the lender when they are first disclosed to you and see if you can whittle down or eliminate some of them.

Last, don't be surprised if your mortgage is sold to another party within months of your home purchase. That won't affect your loan or the loan's terms. But you may write the first couple of checks to one company and the subsequent checks to another. Nearly all mortgages are sold these days—sometimes several times—and it can be a challenge to remember where to send the check.

ADDITIONAL DIRECTIONS

A number of financial Web sites, including www.HSH.com, Yahoo!, Smart Money, and www.Bankrate.com, offer morgage calculators and other worksheets so you can see how varying interest rates and home costs will affect your monthly payment.

Map: a Quick Monthly Payment Chart

DIVIDE YOUR LOAN AMOUNT BY $1.000.
FIND THE INTEREST RATE AND MULTIPLY
BY THE RELEVANT NUMBER TO SEE YOUR
MONTHLY PAYMENT.

Interest rate %	15-year loan	30-year loan	Interest rate %	15-year loan	30-year loan
4.00	$ 7.40	$ 4.77	7.00	$ 8.99	$ 6.65
4.25	7.52	4.92	7.25	9.13	6.82
4.50	7.65	5.07	7.50	9.27	6.99
4.75	7.78	5.22	7.75	9.41	7.16
5.00	7.91	5.37	8.00	9.56	7.34
5.25	8.04	5.52	8.25	9.70	7.51
5.50	8.17	5.68	8.50	9.85	7.69
5.75	8.30	5.84	8.75	9.99	7.87
6.00	8.44	6.00	9.00	10.14	8.05
6.25	8.57	6.16	9.25	10.29	8.23
6.50	8.71	6.32	9.50	10.44	8.41
6.75	8.85	6.49	9.75	10.59	8.59
			10.00	10.75	8.78

Source: *The Wall Street Journal. Complete Finance Guidebook* by Jeff D. Opdyke; copyright © by Dow Jones & Company. Used by permission of Three Rivers Press, a division of Random House, Inc.

Homeowner's Insurance

Protect your biggest asset.

MAP IT

If you borrow to buy a house, your lender will require you to have homeowner's insurance to protect its investment. Even without a mortgage, you'd want to insure your home. But not all policies are the same.

Your policy will help you repair or rebuild your home if it is damaged or destroyed, such as if a nearby tree tumbles onto it in a storm. The policy should also cover your personal belongings, protect you in case someone is hurt on your property, and pick up your living expenses if a fire or broken pipe makes your home unlivable.

The face amount of your policy will typically be less than what you paid for the house, especially in high-cost areas. That's because the policy doesn't need to include the value of the land.

DIRECTIONS

As with renter's insurance, you'll want to know the premium, or annual cost, and the deductible. A standard policy should cover the estimated cost of the dwelling and personal items up to 50 percent to 70 percent of the house cost.

In other words, if your house structure is insured for $150,000, your clothes, furniture, and pots and pans are insured for $75,000 to $105,000. If you need more coverage for valuable items, you'll need to buy it. Your belongings should also be covered when you travel.

Ask the insurance company to walk you through exactly what is covered and for how much. Jewelry, fine art, collectibles, and other valuables may have coverage limits and therefore require additional insurance specifically for those.

You also need to know how much liability coverage you have if you are sued after someone falls on your walkway or slides down your staircase or if your dog bites a neighbor. You may want to raise this number if you feel like the coverage wouldn't adequately protect you in a lawsuit.

Insurance rates vary by state, but homeowner's insurance typically runs from $500 to $1,000 per year, more in coastal states that are prone to hurricanes.

THE DIRECT ROUTE

Since prices can vary widely, you will want to shop around. You may want to start with the company that already insures your car.

As with renter's and car insurance, a higher deductible can cut your costs—but only if you're comfortable with paying the first $1,000 or more in potential damages yourself.

At the least, your home and your personal property should be insured for their replacement value rather than for their current value. That is, the actual value of your clothes may be just a few hundred dollars today but they would cost a lot more than that to replace if they were destroyed. You'll be better off with a *guaranteed replacement cost* or an *extended replacement cost* policy, which will ensure that your stuff will be replaced even if the cost turns out to be higher than your policy limits. It will be more expensive, but it could protect you if construction costs soar.

If your policy isn't automatically adjusted for inflation, every few years you need to be sure that you are carrying enough insurance to cover the costs of materials and construction.

Only the federal government provides insurance for floods. If you live in an area that is susceptible to a flood, you may need to buy separate flood insurance. See www.FloodSmart. gov for more information.

If you were to lose your house to a fire, you would have to create an inventory of everything you lost. To have a record of your things, some experts recommend videotaping each room in your house or taking digital pictures, and then storing them in a safe-deposit box or fireproof safe. The insurance industry also has a home-inventory Web site, www.KnowYourStuff.org.

Ask your insurer if you qualify for discounts for having smoke detectors, a security system, fire extinguishers, or certain kinds of locks or electrical systems.

One-Time Big-Ticket Purchases

Research and persistence can pay off on pricier items.

MAP IT

Somewhere between the modest cost of a camera and the staggering cost of a new car are a host of life necessities that can cost $1,000 or more: a decent sofa, a computer, a refrigerator, mattresses and beds, jewelry, and even big-screen TVs.

Without some planning, these purchases can be real budget busters. After all, few will last a decade or more, so you don't want to spend years paying for them. Yet they are pricey enough that it may be hard to pay cash up front without some planning and budgeting. If you do finance them, you'll pay at the highest rates, using credit cards or store financing at interest rates that can exceed 20 percent.

Because the outlay is significant, you'll want to be sure to pick a sturdy, well-made model and get a fair deal.

DIRECTIONS

Shopping around for big-ticket items is crucial. If you are looking for an appliance or electronic item, figure out the specific models with the features you want and search the Internet by model number to find typical prices. It's not uncommon for prices to vary by as much as 20 percent.

When comparing store prices and Internet prices, take into account shipping and handling costs and whether you'll be paying sales tax. In addition, consider what other accessories will be required for your new purchase to work. Will you need cables for the new TV or computer? New sheets to fit on that much-deeper mattress? A stain-resistant coating to protect the sofa from your puppy?

Sofas, mattresses, and jewelry are notoriously difficult to comparison shop for, so it helps to look at several variations to get a sense of the going rate and what to expect at various price tags.

Ratings from *Consumer Reports* and online services like CNET.com can help you narrow your choices, separate the gems from the junk, and highlight the features that are most important to you.

THE DIRECT ROUTE

Once you do your homework, set a budget. There are always more and less expensive models, so it will help to know your range and how you plan to pay for the purchase before you shop.

In most cases, the cheapest big-ticket purchase isn't always the best. The least expensive models may be far less durable or the electronics may grow outdated faster than a midpriced offering. You could find yourself replacing the bargain buy in just a few years and spending more than you would have if you'd gone with the more advanced option in the first place. You may be better off with a higher-quality, gently used product or a family hand-me-down while you save up for your own new version. It's better to wait until you can invest in something that will make the cost worthwhile than to spend on a low-quality option.

With any big purchase, it helps to negotiate. If you are buying two or more pieces of furniture, for instance, you may get a discount. And even if you don't get a price break, you may get free delivery, free or discounted accessories, or other breaks. It never hurts to ask.

Avoid extended warranties. These have become huge profit centers for stores, which know that most items won't break down in the first few years—and that it's hard for customers to keep track of the paperwork. If an item does fall apart just after the manufacturer's warranty expires, call the manufacturer and make your case. Depending on the product and the manufacturer, you may be able to get a replacement or repair.

Be skeptical of special financing offers of "no interest" or "no payments" for a period of time. If you are extremely disciplined and are sure you will pay the bill before interest and payments kick in, you might save a little money. But there are many loopholes.

➤ You may have to have a high credit score to qualify.

➤ The retailer may be artificially raising the purchase price to justify the financing.

➤ This financing may, in fact, be a new credit card with a limit near the purchase price. That additional "maxed-out" credit could affect your credit score.

➤ Every payment must be on time to avoid penalties. For example, a "no payments for six months" offer will require that a purchase made in January be paid in full before August 1. If you still owe even a small amount when that date rolls around, you'll pay interest charges on the whole purchase going back to January.

Case in point: A "no interest for 36 months" offer from Best Buy requires that buyers make minimum monthly payments on a new Best Buy credit card. Any missed payments will result in all interest charges being assessed—at an annual rate of 21.9 percent to 24.9 percent. Moreover, late payments may trigger an even higher interest rate.

If the bill isn't fully paid at thirty-six months, interest will be charged going back to the purchase date. If you can't pay cash, you may well be better off charging the purchase on a low-interest credit card and paying it off as quickly as possible.

PART IV

SPENDING IT:
THE LITTLE STUFF

Life isn't about penny-pinching. Sure, you can clip coupons from the Sunday newspaper and save on groceries, or only frequent the dollar-movie theater. But what's the point?

You work hard to earn money. A good portion of it has to go to basics, like rent, transportation, and food. Some needs to go to savings, and maybe to charity. But there should be something left for a few things that you want, for stuff that is really fun or entertaining or that makes you happy.

Still, even when you treat yourself, you can be practical about it. You can shop around for good deals and consider the various options. This section tries to help you do that by offering ways to make smart choices on the smaller expenses that can add up quickly, like cell phones, gym memberships, and pet needs. It might even help you find some money in the form of a gift card that has been in your drawer since your birthday five years ago.

WATER, HEAT, TV

Individually or bundled, utility bills can add up.

MAP IT

Household services are hidden costs that can be easy to forget about. But depending on where you live and whether you rent or own, you may have to pay monthly for crucial services like water and sewage service, electricity, natural gas, and trash pickup.

You may also want landline telephone service, digital subscriber line (DSL), cable or satellite TV, and a security system. You can count on a minimum of $20 or $25 a month for each of them—and often more—potentially adding a couple of hundred dollars to your monthly expenses.

DIRECTIONS

When you rent, your landlord should be able to tell you the utility providers in your area and what you'll need to sign up for. If there are multiple providers of, say, electricity or security systems, you can ask your new neighbors which ones have worked out the best.

If you don't have a credit record or if your credit is poor, utility providers can require a deposit, typically equal to one or two months' bills. You likely will also pay installation or other start-up fees, substantially adding to your move-in costs.

Not surprisingly, many service providers will also try to sell you extras along with the basics. The telephone company may push add-ons like call waiting or caller ID at an additional monthly cost, and the cable or satellite people will offer movie or sports packages. They may be enticing—and useful—but you'll need to know the costs, taxes included, to figure out if you can afford them.

THE DIRECT ROUTE

Before you begin signing up for services, make a list of what you really need. If you want a telephone landline, will you be making mostly local calls or will you be calling long distance? If your cell phone has plenty of free night and weekend minutes, will you be better off making long-distance calls from it? Do you need other services like DSL—or is wireless available where you live?

Telephone and cable companies in particular may try to sell you "bundles" of goodies, combining, for instance, local and long-distance service, DSL, television services, and even cellular services all on one bill. If you were going to buy all those separately anyway, the bundle might save you a fair bit of money. But you could also end up paying for services you don't need or want. Check out the options on the providers' Web sites and do the math before you get an enthusiastic salesperson on the phone.

Avoid deposits if you can. Companies may ask a parent or someone else to cosign with you to avoid a deposit. If you must pay one, try to negotiate a smaller deposit, and ask when it will be returned. Some companies return them after a year if you pay your bills on time; others use deposits to pay your last bill.

If you get behind on your bills, don't just ignore them. Call the company and try to work out a payment plan. Paying your bills in smaller increments over time may cost you some interest but it is much cheaper than having your service cut off, which can result in additional fees, dings on your credit record, and new charges to fire up the service again.

When you move, be sure that all the utility companies have your new address and phone number so that you don't leave any outstanding bills. The utility company may also need that information to return any deposits you made.

Renter's Insurance

Protecting your stuff and your assets.

MAP IT

You may not think you own much. But if you have a computer, some furniture, and clothes for four seasons, replacing them all could cost you a bundle.

If you rent, your landlord will have insurance covering the structure. But unless you buy renter's insurance, your stuff won't be covered if it is stolen or damaged by fire or the water from a busted pipe. In addition, renter's insurance can protect you if someone falls or is hurt in your apartment.

In the grand scheme of costs, renter's insurance is relatively cheap, typically between $150 and $250 a year, or $15 to $20 a month.

DIRECTIONS

To buy the insurance, you can check online or call around to the best-known insurance companies. You'll want to ask:

➤ What's the premium, or the annual cost per year?

➤ What's the deductible, or the amount you have to pay per year before the insurance kicks in?

➤ What is covered under the policy? Are computers fully covered? What about big televisions or fine jewelry?

➤ What kinds of damages are covered—and what aren't? For instance, if you're in an earthquake-prone area, is earthquake damage covered?

➤ Are your personal items covered when you are traveling?

➤ If your apartment is unlivable, will the insurance cover your cost to stay somewhere else?

➤ How much coverage do you need? You may have to estimate the total value of all your household goods.

➤ How much liability coverage will you have in case something happens to someone else in your apartment? Will the insurance company pay for your defense if you're sued?

THE DIRECT ROUTE

As with any insurance, you'll want to shop around a little. Most well-known insurers offer renter's insurance. If you have car insurance already, the same company may offer renter's insurance to you on a single bill. You may also want to try the insurance company your parents use.

If you're willing to have a higher deductible—say $500 or $1,000 instead of $250—you can cut the annual premium.

While it's more expensive, you'll want to insure your personal property for the replacement cost, not the actual value today. That is, the actual value of your sofa may be just $100 today but it would cost more than that to replace if it were destroyed.

Cell Phones

Talk is not cheap.

MAP IT

The cell-phone industry has your number: It knows that younger customers like the newest phones, text regularly, and use their cell phones more than landlines. And the industry is thrilled to charge mightily for all of it.

Your provider also wants to keep you around, so it offers the best deals on phones and service to those who agree to one- or two-year contracts. Still, even with attractive rates, your monthly bill can rival your car payment if you don't pay attention to how much you talk on the phone, how many text messages you send and receive, and how many extras you download.

To keep your cell phone bill from draining your bank account, you will need to do a little research and planning before you buy.

DIRECTIONS

The latest cell phones and their features are often the big attraction. But that's only part of a complex cost equation that may leave you longing for the simplicity of high-school algebra. Because you may be locked into a contract for a long time, you also need to be sure that you've picked a good service and a plan that works for your budget.

Cell-phone plans come in three main flavors:

Long-term Plans. You pay a fixed monthly rate and commit to a contract that's typically two years. These plans are best for moderate to heavy phone users because they start with a fairly high number of weekday minutes. They offer the lowest per-minute rates, the best prices on phones, and often the best selection of phone choices. For big-time texters or those who use their phones for e-mail or the Internet, additional packages can cut the per-message cost of those services—but add to your total bill.

These plans may also offer unlimited night-and-weekend minutes separately from the minutes that are part of your plan, though that perk may be less attractive than it seems; nighttime begins at 7 p.m. for some carriers and at 9 p.m. for others. Some plans offer unlimited free calling to other cell phones using the same carrier.

The disadvantages? You make a hefty, long-term commitment (see "Contracts," page 56). You'll need a decent credit score to qualify and there are hidden costs, like activation fees. Surcharges and federal, state, and local taxes can easily add $10 or more to your monthly bill, making a $40 service cost $50 or more. In addition, you may pay a termination fee of $150 to $200 per line if you cancel the agreement early.

"Prepaid" Plans. You pay a fixed rate every month for a set number of minutes. Your monthly charge is debited from your checking account or charged to a credit card. These plans make the most sense for light to moderate users.

Phone choices are somewhat limited, phone prices may be higher, and you have to pay up front to keep the phone working if you use up your minutes. Per-minute charges are also somewhat higher. Depending on your state, you may pay only sales tax on the plan or additional taxes and surcharges.

Still, you avoid a long contract as well as activation and termination fees and you don't pay for a lot of minutes that you aren't using.

Pay-as-You-Go Plans. These are the phones and plans you find in convenience stores, drugstores, and other outlets. Overall, they are among the most costly per-minute and have the fewest phone choices. They also have some tricky features. You may pay $1 each day you use the phone, in addition to 10¢ or more per minute. You "refill" the phone with a phone card or by buying more minutes from the carrier. But some refills can expire in as little as thirty days—and you lose any unused balance.

These plans make the most sense for people who use their phones only for emergencies and for those with tight budgets who need to keep their calls to a minimum. If you find yourself spending more than $50 a month for your service, you will probably be better off on a monthly plan.

What does service cost for a moderate user? The chart below compares the costs of four different plans offered by AT&T in fall 2008 for a New Yorker who wants about 400 minutes a month of weekday service:

Map: The Cost of Cell Phone Service

Features	Contract plan	"Prepaid" plan	Pay-as-you-go 1	Pay-as-you-go 2
Monthly fee	$39.99	$49.99	Approx $65	Approx $100
Number of weekday minutes	450	400	400	400
Cost per minute	9¢	12.5 cents	$1 per day of phone use, plus 10¢/minute	25¢
Night/weekend minutes*	5,000	3,000	unlimited for $19.99 extra	25¢/minute
Estimated taxes	$8.95	$4.20	$5.45	$8.38
Activation fee	$36	0	0	0
Termination fee	$175	0	0	0
Text messages, sent and received	20¢ each	20¢ each	20¢ each	20¢ each
Cheapest text package	$5 for 200; unlimited to AT&T users	$4.99 for 200	$4.99 for 200	$4.99 for 200
Additional daytime minutes	45¢/ minute	12.5¢/ minute	10¢/ minute	25¢/ minute
Contract length	2 years	—	—	—
Calls to other AT&T customers	Unlimited	Unlimited	Unlimited	25¢/minute
Total monthly cost with text package, taxes	Approx. $55	Approx. $60	Approx. $76	Approx. $114

*Nights start at 9 p.m.

The chart above covers only some of the fees. You'll pay at least a dollar or two for each ring tone or wallpaper you download (and maybe ongoing monthly fees), $1.79 or more for each call to directory assistance, and additional amounts for downloading games.

To compare plans from different providers or different levels of service, make your own chart, focusing on the features that are most important or relevant to you:

Features				
Monthly cost				
Number of weekday minutes				
Cost per minute				
Night/Weekend minutes				
Estimated taxes				
Activation fee				
Termination fee				
Text messages, sent and received				
Text package				
Additional daytime minutes				
Other services				
Contract length				
Mobile to mobile calls				
Total monthly cost with text package, taxes				

THE DIRECT ROUTE

Here are strategies to simplify what has become a painfully complicated process:

➤ Pay attention to service first. A recent *Consumer Reports* survey found that the main reasons people switch service providers or gripe about their phones are dropped calls and dead spots. Poll your friends, neighbors, and coworkers to find out which services work best at home, school, or at work. You may even be able to borrow a phone from a store to try it out on your usual routes.

➤ Once you narrow down the service providers, look for the phones and plans you want. Estimate the weekday minutes you use each month and add 10 percent to 20 percent as a cushion. You'll pay a big penalty for going over your allotted minutes in a given month, forking over 25¢ to 45¢ a minute. You are almost certainly better off paying for a package with extra minutes built in.

➤ If you stay in one place, a regional or local plan may be far cheaper than one with free nationwide calling. If you travel with the phone, though, you will pay extra roaming charges and heftier per-minute charges.

➤ Fashionable phones are fun, but so are handsets that fit your needs. Are the keys comfortable and easy to use? Is the screen easy to read? How long will the battery go without recharging, and how long can you talk before the phone dies? Is the price in your budget?

➤ Beyond that, do you need a camera? Music? Internet access? Bluetooth?

➤ Do the math to see if other packages make sense. If you send or receive 100 text messages a month, you may pay $20 a month, depending on what the carrier charges. A package of 200 messages per month will be cheaper. If you text a lot, an unlimited package may save you a lot of money.

➤ If you get along well with roommates or close friends, consider joining up to get a family plan. You'll share a pool of minutes, but you both may share a lot of saved money, too.

➤ Negotiate. The cell-phone provider may waive the activation fee or throw in a battery charger for your car for free.

You might get free thirty-day trials of texting or game packages. But you may not know that unless you ask.

➤ Ask questions about what your monthly bill will look like, including taxes and other surcharges, so that you aren't surprised later. The business has become so complex that the carriers often include a section on their Web sites on how to read their bills.

➤ Understand the trial period. Most companies will give you two weeks to a month in which you can get out of the deal if the phone or the service isn't working well for you. After that, you're on the hook for the termination fee if you end the contract.

➤ While changing cell-phone companies can be difficult once you're under contract, you can still change your plan if you need more minutes—or fewer—or if you want to add other services. You may also be able to swap for a new phone before your contract is up. If you do, however, find out if the company requires you to extend your contract for two more years.

➤ If you go for a prepaid or pay-as-you-go plan, be sure you can check your balance from your phone or online so that you know how many minutes you have left. Also check expiration dates on refills so that you don't lose any of your money.

➤ Don't buy what you don't need. If you lose your phone, you'll probably have to pay the full retail price—rather than a discounted price—to replace it. Replacement insurance costs about $5 a month, or $60 a year, and requires a $50 deductible, so you may spend more than $100 up front before you replace your phone. It may be cheaper to skip the insurance and try to buy a replacement on eBay or another Web site. (Before you buy, however, be sure the phone will work with your service provider.)

ADDITIONAL DIRECTIONS

Consumer Reports (www.ConsumerReports.org), CNET (www.CNET.com), and J. D. Power (www.JDPower.com) rate cellphone companies and telephones.

To compare telephones and services, try www.MyRatePlan.com, www.PhoneDog.com, www.LetsTalk.com, or www.PhoneScoop.com.

Joining a Gym

Killer abs shouldn't kill your budget.

MAP IT

Working out is an important part of a healthy lifestyle, and belonging to a clean, well-maintained fitness center can make staying in shape easier to do. But joining a health club or gym is another monthly chunk out of the budget and can sometimes be an adventure in frustration and negotiation.

While joining and leaving some gyms is a snap, health clubs in general are notorious for using high-pressure sales tactics. They'll tell you that special discounts are about to expire and some may try to convince you to agree to two- or three-year memberships that are hard to cancel. Others may try to sell you buckets of expensive personal-training services, online nutrition trackers, and even vitamins and other supplements.

Even if you think you're getting a good deal now, in a year or two, you could find yourself still paying a monthly fee for a gym that is far from home or that no longer serves your needs. A gym that's a good match should be happy to have you for the short term as well as the long term.

DIRECTIONS

A fitness or health club worth joining should be convenient to your home or work. If it's a hassle to get to or off your beaten path, you'll find more excuses to skip a visit.

Also be sure that your facility opens early enough or closes late enough to accommodate your exercise schedule. If you like to work out on the weekends, are the hours convenient for you? Do the classes offered fit in to your schedule?

While looking for clubs that have the classes, equipment, and facilities that match your interests, keep in mind that you'll probably pay more for more amenities. Would you like a swimming pool? Racquetball courts? A basketball court? A steam room or sauna? Child care? And if you don't, do you need to pay for a gym that offers all of them?

If you want to work with a personal trainer, ask about the trainers' qualifications. What kind of certification do they have? How much do they charge and how available are they? Can you pay by the workout, or do you have to sign up for several sessions at a time? It also helps to know if the trainers are gym employees or independent contractors. The fitness center may take responsibility for a problem with an employee, but wash its hands of issues with a contractor.

When you tour the facility, look for out-of-order machines; several of them could be a sign that the facility isn't maintained well. You should also check out the locker room to see if it's clean, scope out where you would put your stuff, and see if the lockers seem secure.

Most fitness clubs require an initiation or joining fee as well as monthly payments. Any agreement you sign should clearly spell out how much you'll pay and when, how long you are committed, and how you can cancel. The agreement should also explain whether you can freeze your membership if you can't exercise for medical reasons or if you leave town for an extended period, and whether you can transfer your membership to someone else if you no longer want it.

Ask yourself, Is this a place where I'll be happy to work out two or three times a week or more?

THE DIRECT ROUTE

Many health clubs will offer a trial membership or at least a day pass so you can try out the facility. Take advantage of that, and visit at the time when you would normally work out to see how crowded it is and whether you'll have to wait for certain machines or equipment.

In addition to chains, check into other alternatives, like community centers and YMCAs and YWCAs, which may have more flexible policies and lower prices.

Once you've done your research and settled on a gym that meets your needs and is in your budget, consider these steps to ease the sign-up process:

➤ Don't rush to sign up because a special promotion is ending. One promotion is nearly always followed by another.

➤ Negotiate. Initiation or joining fees are often flexible, and you may be able to reduce your up-front cost.

➤ Before you sign anything, be sure you understand how much you are to pay, how and when the payment is due, and how the contract will end. Do you need to notify someone in writing to cancel? How many days in advance must the letter be sent? What will you owe at that time? Some gyms charge you up front for the first and last months of payment—but you may still owe another month when you cancel.

➤ Find out if the contract renews automatically and when that happens, so that you can stop it if you need to.

➤ It's a good idea to take home a contract and read it before signing. Once you have signed it, be sure to get a copy and keep it in case there are any problems later.

➤ Try out the gym and watch the trainers in action before committing to multiple workouts. And be skeptical of anyone pushing vitamins, supplements, or other nutritional aids. Chances are their enthusiasm for the products is largely driven by the commissions they receive on the sales.

➤ If you change your mind, you probably can cancel the membership within three to five days of signing without penalty, depending on your state's consumer laws. After that, though, you're stuck with the contract.

➤ Many gyms want to automatically deduct your monthly payment from your bank or credit card, and that may be a convenient way to go. If possible, choose a credit card. That way you might be able to dispute the charges if the club closes or there's a problem later on.

➤ If you want personal training, you may want to hire a trainer directly and bypass a gym membership. Similarly, if yoga is all you want, look for a place that charges only for the classes you take. Or if you use a fitness center sporadically, consider going à la carte and simply buying day passes. You may also be able to take over someone else's membership if you don't want to commit for a year or two. (Check Craigslist or classified ads.) And you can always just find a friend who will walk or run with you regularly, or look for biking or hiking clubs that take regular excursions.

➤ If your company reimburses you for fitness expenses, find out what the requirements are and get the necessary paperwork from your gym.

Owning Pets

They're cuddly, adorable, and expensive.

MAP IT

There are few companions in the world more wonderful than an adoring pet, or few things better than coming home after a hard day at work to the unconditional love of a four-legged friend.

But just like partners and children, pets have their needs: food, medical care, and 24/7 housing. And none of it is free. Moreover, only you can provide it. Before you fall head over heels in love with a furry dependent, consider how you will pay and provide for your new pal.

DIRECTIONS

Maybe you'll get your pet for free. Maybe you'll pay hundreds of dollars for the breed you want most. Either way, the initial cost of a dog, cat, or any other animal is only the tip of the tail when it comes to the total outlay.

First stop: the vet. The average cost of an exam, shots, and heartworm medicine for a cat or dog is about $150 to $200. Spaying or neutering could cost up to $400 depending on the size of the animal and where you go.

You'll also need the basics: bowls, a collar, a leash or litter box, a bed, and maybe a crate or carrier, which can easily add up to more than $100, depending on your tastes.

Food will run you at least $150 to $350 a year, on the lower end for smaller animals and on the high end for big ones. Specialty foods or those for dogs or cats on special diets can cost $500 or more. Vitamins and treats are extra.

Grooming can be something like your own haircuts, $35 or more per visit, or $200 to $400 a year.

Just those basics add up to roughly $1,000 a year, and up to 50 percent more for a big dog.

Then, there are the less obvious costs: Your landlord may charge you a larger security deposit and possibly higher rent for a pet—and some landlords won't allow pets at all. You'll need to commit time to walking your dog, playing with your animal, or keeping an eye out for it, which cuts into time you have for other things.

You'll also need a plan for when you're not home. Friends may not always be available to pet-sit. Boarding often starts at $20 a night, but can be much more than that, especially on holidays and weekends.

The real wild card is your pet's health. Allergies can require visits to a specialist and special medicines. A challenging pet with a penchant for eating bizarre things or jumping through plate-glass windows can end up in the pet emergency clinic regularly, adding hundreds and even thousands of dollars to your annual costs.

Finally, there are unexpected or end-of-life illnesses, when you may have to decide whether to pay hundreds or thousands of dollars more to extend your animal's life. If you don't have that kind of savings, you'll have to make a difficult decision whether to take on debt for a sick pet.

THE DIRECT ROUTE

Shortcuts here are few and far between, though you can control some expenses by keeping a leash on purchases of toys, pet accessories, and other extras.

For low-cost spaying or neutering, vaccinations, or other services, contact your local Humane Society or animal shelter. Some will also offer student discounts.

When you need a veterinarian, ask friends for referrals. You'll want a vet who is near where you live, with convenient hours and good options for emergency situations. Collect two or three names and compare prices, which can vary widely. You may also want to see what retail pet stores charge for vaccinations.

Pet insurance may be an unnecessary extra. Most pets won't need it, and it may not cover certain conditions. Be sure you know what will and won't be covered before signing up.

If you crave animal companionship but cost is a big concern, fish, hamsters, and small birds are the cheapest choices, though far less cuddly on a cold night.

ADDITIONAL DIRECTIONS

The American Society for the Prevention of Cruelty to Animals Web site has information on choosing pets and their costs, www.ASPCA.org.

GIFT GIVING

Finding the right mix of manners and money.

MAP IT

The invitations come rolling in: Your good friends are getting engaged, married, and having babies. All of a sudden you have a list of gifts to buy that you haven't worked into your budget. Even if your bank account is running on the light side, you can't ignore them; some long-time relationships may be at stake. And even if you can easily afford to be generous, how much to spend and on what can be baffling.

Steering through these potential land mines can take some creativity. You'll need to find the right combination of proper etiquette and clever ideas to keep from busting your budget and to keep friends and relatives happy.

DIRECTIONS

First, the rules of the game: An invitation is not a demand for a gift. True, a wedding invitation does call for a nice present for the bride and groom. But for the most part, whether you give a gift and how generous you are depends on your relationship with the person involved, your personal budget, and your background. In this case, what your mother taught you may really matter.

Here are more details:

Showers. Bridal and baby showers are intended to help the newlyweds and new parents get going. If you are invited and attend, you should bring a gift. Whether you spend $20 or $200 is less important than whether the gift is useful and something the recipients will like.

Generally, you should spend less on a shower gift than on the wedding gift. If you can't attend the shower, you don't have to send a gift. Presumably, you will be sending a wedding gift or baby gift later.

Engagement Parties. Whether a gift is expected when a couple's engagement is celebrated varies by region. If it's your custom or common in your area, you can bring or send something small, like a cookbook, a bottle of wine, or a picture frame.

Weddings. If you are invited to a wedding, you probably know the bride or groom pretty well, and a gift should be sent, even if you can't attend. Again, the thought matters more than the money spent. A set of ice cream bowls or picnic supplies can be just as pleasing as an expensive place setting.

Hosts and Hostesses. In some parts of the country, it's considered rude to show up for a dinner party empty-handed. If you aren't sure, ask around, or err on the safe side. You don't need to spend a lot. A small plant, a decent bottle of wine, or a box of candy can be found for $10 or less. For a casual gathering, a bag of chips or a dip may be sufficient.

However, if you are a houseguest, you should definitely bring your host a small gift. And if you stay for more than a couple of days, you should treat your hosts to dinner out or make a meal. After all, you are saving a bundle by not having to stay in a hotel—and you might want to be invited back.

Children. If you are regularly invited to the birthday party of a relative or a friend's child, the kiddo will come to expect a gift from you—even if you can't attend. Young kids, however, rarely care about prices. A good book, a fun card game, and just about anything that bounces or makes an obnoxious noise will do the trick.

Bosses. Giving the boss a birthday or holiday gift can leave the impression that you're trying to win favor, both with the boss and other colleagues. Some companies may have rules forbidding that practice. But it may be customary in other offices.

Certainly, you don't owe your boss a gift or a card. But if your coworkers want to go in together on a gift, that may be a safe option. Or a card or a birthday cake from the group should be plenty.

Thank-yous. When someone goes out of the way to help you out, a small gift is a nice way to say thanks. A book, a gift card, or food show appreciation to someone who took care of you when you were sick, bailed you out when you needed an extra set of hands, or spent a day helping you move.

THE DIRECT ROUTE

Gifts should never break your budget or leave you in debt. They just aren't important enough to justify ruining your finances.

The best way to keep gift spending under control is to set a firm budget for what you can spend on any specific gift or holiday and stick to it. Holidays can be especially tough because you can so easily be tempted to buy one or two more things. If you have trouble staying close to your budget, try withdrawing cash for your budgeted amount and spending only that on your gifts. When the cash is gone, your shopping is over.

A book with a personal message, a handmade item, or something put together just for a friend—like photos, recipes, or advice for the new couple—may be treasured more than an expensive gift.

If you are worried about buying the right kind of gift for a friend's wedding or baby, ask someone else to go in with you. Putting two small budgets together may help you find a present you feel good about.

You don't have to buy from a couple's wedding or baby registry. Look at what they have listed, however, to see what has already been purchased and to get an idea of what they would like. Then use those ideas as a springboard for something more personal.

If you are invited to multiple showers for the same person, you don't have to bring a gift to each one. Figure out how much you want to spend on the shower gift and then decide whether to do it all at once or in pieces. You can bring one nice gift to one of the showers, or small gifts to all of them, like candlesticks to one shower and candles to another.

It's perfectly okay to spend different amounts on different people. You certainly are going to spend more on a close relative or best friend than on a distant relative or family acquaintance.

Office gift giving can be unusually awkward. Whether you make a donation for an office gift and how much should be voluntary. If the collector is hovering, tell him or her that you're busy and that you'll bring the envelope back shortly; you shouldn't be pressured into giving more than you want to contribute—and you shouldn't have to donate at all.

WRONG TURNS

Gift giving isn't very difficult, but there are some areas to watch out for:

➤ Cut flowers for hosts are lovely, but they should come with a vase. Asking a host to stop, find a container, and clip flowers when you arrive isn't the best way to start a dinner party.

➤ Before you bring alcohol as a gift, be sure it will be welcome. If you aren't certain that a person drinks, consider bringing something else. This is doubly true if the event is office related, like a party at the boss's house.

➤ The practice called regifting—wrapping up a gift you have received and giving it to someone else—is tacky. No way around it. The best thing to do with a gift you cannot return is to offer it to someone else unwrapped and with full disclosure. But if you feel compelled to wrap it up and call it a gift, make sure all the personal tags have been removed and keep it in the original packaging. You should also consider how the original giver and the recipient would react if they found out.

➤ Last, thank-you notes never go out of style. If someone gives you a nice gift, a handwritten thank you is the proper response. However, if you aren't likely to ever pull out a piece of paper and find a stamp, an e-mail thank-you is much better than no thank-you at all.

Vacations

Give yourself a break.

MAP IT

Vacations are one of the reasons you work. Whether you take time off to hang out at home, visit friends, or see some exotic locale, they're good for the heart and the head.

But they can also be tough on the pocketbook. Unleashed from the job and basking in some faraway place, you may throw caution to the wind, indulging in fancy meals and splurging on souvenirs that you don't really need. Only when you return and see all the bills together is it clear what a financial mess you've made. What happens in Vegas may stay there, but the credit-card charges will surely follow you home.

A little foresight, a realistic budget, and some travel tips can keep you from having to work overtime to pay for your vacation foibles.

DIRECTIONS

Start with a budget in mind. In theory, you should save up for your trips so that they're essentially paid for when you return. More realistically, you shouldn't spend more than you can pay off in the next month or two. By then, you may be ready for another expedition.

For a simple getaway, see the following chapters for tips and tricks on buying plane tickets, booking hotels, and renting cars.

For a ski trip, an excursion overseas, or another destination vacation, you may save money with an all-in-one deal, but you'll have to price it out. It's quite possible that a package including airfare, hotel, and lift tickets could save you hundreds of dollars over what you might pay if you booked each separately—and it would save you time as well. Be aware, though, that even if you end up on your regular airline, you may not get frequent-flier miles or credit for your hotel reward program when you book package deals.

To see what's available, check newspaper travel sections and airline Web sites for their vacation deals as well as the packages on popular travel Web sites like Orbitz, Expedia, and Travelocity. (Another, Kayak, pulls together prices from numerous sites.) While you're there, you can compare the price to the cost if you booked each piece separately. Always make your reservations with a credit card, just in case there's a problem later.

Some cruises also offer package deals that include airfare and transportation to and from the boat. If you're interested in a cruise, book early, before the cheap fares sell out, or wait until the last minute, when unsold cabins may be available for a song. And be prepared to spend a lot more than your initial cost for excursions off the boat, soft or hard drinks on the boat, and significant tips for everyone from your waiter to the person who tidies your room.

You can book excursions through the cruise company, but you may save a lot of money booking on your own via the Internet or waiting until you get to the port.

To see if other travelers have any advice, you can also run your planned trip through a search engine to see if others' experiences generated many comments.

THE DIRECT ROUTE

Vacations are a good thing. Take time off, and within reason, go somewhere exciting or interesting and have fun.

Nowadays, you may pay for the airfare and hotel up front, so much of the trip's cost will be clear before you leave. For shorter trips, take cash for the rest of your expenses so you know exactly how much you can spend. For longer trips, use your debit card to get cash that you've budgeted. Bring a credit card, but use it only for emergencies.

If you're traveling overseas, wait until you get to your destination to get cash in the local currency. Then use your debit card at an ATM. Depending on your bank and your credit-card provider, you may pay additional foreign-currency transaction fees on each transaction.

If you are looking for something specific, a travel agent may be the best way to get a good deal. The time and money you save could easily cover the commission you'll pay.

For more travel information see "Air Travel," page 195; "Hotels," page 199; "Rental Cars," page 202; and "Tipping," page 205.

AIR TRAVEL

You can go anywhere—if the rules don't trip you up.

MAP IT

A proliferation of discount airlines has made air travel more accessible to many consumers—if you know how to play the game. The problem is that many airlines have more rules than a high-school hall monitor, and you need to know them to get the best deals and avoid extra fees.

Luckily, the Internet has made shopping around relatively easy. And if you're willing to be a flexible traveler, you can find good deals to just about anywhere.

DIRECTIONS

Airfare prices change all the time, so today's price may be higher or lower tomorrow. Generally, the earlier you book a trip, the better fare you'll get. But you may also snare bargains if you're able to take advantage of last-minute specials.

Finding cheap fares can require some sleuthing. Internet sites Travelocity, Orbitz, and Expedia function like online travel agencies, scouting various airlines for the latest offers. The airlines' own Web sites may also offer fares that aren't available anywhere else, so you'll want to check those as well. And sites like Kayak (for domestic travel) and Mobissimo (for international travel) may smoke out deals you won't find elsewhere.

When comparing fares, be sure taxes and other fees are included. Some travel sites show them right away while others don't add them in until you choose your flight and start to reserve it. Those taxes and fees can significantly change the total cost of a trip.

Some airlines let you put a reservation on hold for about a day, but the price can change or the flight can sell out in the meantime.

If you buy the ticket right away, you have only a day to cancel or change your flight without penalty. After that, beware: Most cheap fares are nonrefundable, meaning you can't get your money back if your plans change. You also can't give your ticket to a friend or relative. If you have to cancel, you can apply the unused amount to a future ticket, but most airlines will charge a $50 to $150 change fee first—and up to $250 for changing international plans. Clearly, it pays to be sure about your plans before you buy.

Generally, to buy a ticket, you'll need a credit card with enough available credit to cover the purchase. Some airlines now accept PayPal, and you can pay cash if you buy the ticket at the airport—though that may subject you to additional security searches.

When you do purchase a ticket, make note of the six-digit confirmation code. You'll need it if you have to change your flight and you may need it to check in at a kiosk at the airport.

Many airlines are now charging for the first or second piece of checked luggage. (Some international discount carriers also charge you to check any luggage.) If your checked bag tops 50 pounds, you'll also be assessed a fee. Each airline's Web site has details on its baggage rules and regulations.

If you check your bag at the curb instead of inside the airport, you'll be expected to tip the baggage handler another dollar or two per bag.

Your luggage should include a tag on the outside with your

name and contact information and another one on the inside, just in case the outside tag is lost.

Security rules for carry-ons can be quirky and can change with short notice. Currently, any liquids that you carry on—from contact lens solution to sunscreen—must meet size restrictions and fit in a quart-sized baggie. You can buy water inside the secured area, but you can't bring in your own. If you haven't flown recently, check the Transportation Security Administration Web site, www.TSA.gov, or your airline's site to see what's allowed and what isn't. This is one area that isn't negotiable.

If you know you aren't going to make a trip, be sure to call and cancel as soon as possible so you can apply your purchase amount to a later ticket. If you know you won't make a flight in time, inform the airline and add your name to a standby list for a later flight. A plane ticket is a bit like a baseball ticket—once the game is underway, the ticket is worthless.

THE DIRECT ROUTE

You'll snare better fares if you are willing to fly early in the morning or late at night instead of in the late afternoon, or if you can travel on Tuesday, Wednesday, or Thursday instead of Friday and Sunday. Want to get home for a holiday? Try flying on Thanksgiving or Christmas Day, instead of just before or after. In addition, connecting flights are usually cheaper than nonstop.

If you fly a route regularly, you'll quickly recognize a good fare when you see it. Snag it when you can because it can change in even a few hours. (If you want to know a historically good fare, www.FareCompare.com can show you the lowest prices in the last month.)

If you fly the same route routinely to go home or see a significant other or do most of your travel on one airline, a frequent-flier program may help you get free flights or other perks. But if your travel is random, you're better off searching for the best fares and not letting brand loyalty drain your wallet.

Students sometimes have trouble figuring out when they

might return home or go back to school, making round-trip planning difficult. Students and others with university e-mail addresses may find better fares and, more important, better one-way fares at two student travel sites: www.StudentUniverse.com and www.STAtravel.com.

If you have to get somewhere right away for an emergency or a funeral, for instance, try a discount carrier, call the airline directly, or go to the airport. You may have to work through several people, but airline agents can waive rules and many will try to work out a way to accommodate you.

If you find the whole process bewildering, call a travel agent. It may cost you an additional $25 or $35, but the agent may save you plenty of money and time and can share advice and expertise that can reduce the hassles and keep your travel fun.

After you've booked your flight, take advantage of airline flight alerts to your cell phone or e-mail. That way you'll know your gate ahead of time and know when to expect delays. If your flight has been canceled, it may be quicker to rebook by calling the airline's 800 number or trying one of its check-in kiosks than by standing in line. You can also check in online up to twenty-four hours before your flight, which may also help you snag a better seat.

If you can navigate the baggie requirements for liquids, carrying on your stuff is usually easier than checking luggage. Most airlines allow one carry-on bag that will fit under the seat or in the overhead bin and one personal item, like a purse or briefcase.

If you need to check luggage, carry on anything you may need for the first twelve or so hours in order to avoid a crisis if your suitcase doesn't arrive when you do. That includes headphones and food, since most airlines only sell snacks these days. You should also carry any important medicines and valuables with you, along with a change of clothes. If your suitcase doesn't show up at the baggage claim, report it right away. You'll have to describe it and maybe the contents. Also ask for a local phone number for the baggage desk since your bag is most likely to arrive someday at that airport.

HOTELS

The high cost of home away from home.

MAP IT

With hotel rooms getting costly in many big cities, you may end up paying more for a few nights' stay than you will in airfare.

The cheapest option, naturally, is to stay with a friend—or find a friend to stay with you in a hotel and split the price. In any event, if you end up at a hotel, expect some hidden costs.

DIRECTIONS

Once again, the Internet can be a huge help in finding a good deal. Hotels.com, as well as the travel sites Orbitz, Expedia, and Travelocity, will search for hotels in specific city locations and at certain rates. If you know where you want to stay or prefer one hotel over another, see if the hotel Web site has better deals.

While you may be tempted to take the cheapest room, reconsider. Safety and location are real issues, so check out the hotel's ratings. If you want to sleep well, you'll want a place that is quiet and well maintained. If you need to use your computer, you'll want free Internet access. If you are arriving late or leaving early in the morning, you may want a restaurant nearby.

And a fitness room or a free pass at a nearby gym may be your only chance to work out during the trip.

The room rate is only part of the equation. In most cities, hotel taxes and fees help support public projects and easily add 10 percent or more to your total cost. Often, you won't know how large the taxes and fees are until you pay the bill.

To make a reservation, you'll need a credit card. Expect the hotel to block out some of your credit—probably for an amount that exceeds your expected bill. Even before you travel, that will limit your available credit for other purchases.

To get the best rates from an online site, you may have to make a nonrefundable payment in advance, with no wiggle room for changes or cancellations. If you have any concerns about whether you will actually make the trip, don't take the risk. Instead, call the hotel or go to its Web site for its best refundable rate or look for a place that will give you a reservation without an up-front payment.

Note the hotel's cancellation rules. Some places allow you to cancel up to the day of the visit without penalty while others require forty-eight hours' notice or more. If you are going to be arriving in the evening, call that day to alert the hotel that you will be late so that it doesn't give someone else your room.

THE DIRECT ROUTE

Generally speaking, weekend rates are cheaper than weekday rates. If you belong to AAA or another travel club, ask if you can get a discount on your rate. You'll pay more downtown than you will at an airport hotel or in a suburban area.

That said, location does matter. If you have to commute an hour to your destination, the cheaper hotel isn't such a great deal. In cities like Boston, Chicago, New York, and Washington, look for spots near subways and other public transportation. It may be worth a little more for a room if you can avoid a bunch of cab fares or the cost of renting a car.

Bring a copy of the reservation with you and a description

of the room, if there is one. That way, if you don't get the room or the rate you booked, you'll have fodder for discussion with the desk clerk or manager.

Room service may look incredibly inviting and it may not seem that expensive. But after gratuities and delivery fees are tacked on, the actual cost is quite high. Similarly, the mini-bar in the room and the soda machine down the hall will likely charge exorbitant prices.

To save money, walk to a place nearby for food or drink. Many pizza places and Chinese restaurants will also deliver to hotels. In fact, the hotel will probably provide a list of those who deliver.

If you need to stay beyond the checkout time, negotiate that in advance. You don't want to inadvertently pay for an extra night.

Rental
Cars

Getting from here to there for less.

MAP IT

A rental car can seem like a big expense—until you compare the rental rate with cab fare to and from the airport.

If you are going to be doing a lot of moving around, a rental car may be the best way to go. Most car-rental companies will rent to those twenty-one years old and older, but they may charge drivers extra until age twenty-five.

Like hotels and air travel, rental cars can include several unexpected fees and costs. Drive carefully.

DIRECTIONS

You can book a car at most travel Web sites and even from most airline sites after you book your flight. Unlike hotels, you rarely have to guarantee your rental with a credit card or pay in advance. But when you pick up the car, the car-rental company may block off a portion of your credit card as security until you return the car and pay for the rental. That could reduce the credit you have available for other things.

As with hotels and planes, there are also plenty of extra

fees. Many cities assess large taxes and fees on rental cars that add on to the daily rate. More and more, companies are showing you those charges when you book the car.

The car-rental company will offer you insurance at a daily rate. If you already have auto insurance, check with your insurance company before you leave to see if you are covered. If so, you can turn down the rental-car offer. But if you don't own a car, you should take the insurance just in case.

You should also have an option to fill up the tank yourself or let them do it for you for a set price. Usually, it's much cheaper for you to buy the gasoline on the way back to the car lot. There's a big penalty for forgetting: You'll be charged a hefty premium if they top off the tank.

If you're directionally challenged and will be doing a lot of destination driving, a GPS navigator can be rented for about $10 a day, which could save you time wandering around, burning expensive gasoline.

When you get the car, check for obvious dents and dings and point them out to the agent so that you won't be charged for them later. If the gas tank isn't full, make sure that is noted as well.

THE DIRECT ROUTE

Rental rates can be all over the map. Sometimes the airport is cheaper; sometimes a suburban location is. Sometimes a corporate rate may save you money; sometimes it doesn't. Generally, weekend rates are cheaper than weekday rates; if you're a AAA or travel club member, ask if there are corresponding discounts.

Reserve a car when you book your travel, but check the rates again before you go. You may find a better deal.

The agent will often try to upgrade you to a bigger car—sometimes because the smaller car isn't available. That's not your problem. If you decline, they still have to provide a car and you should get an upgrade for free.

Check the hours of the rental location. Not all of them are open twenty-four hours, and if you have an early flight, you want to be sure you can return the car.

Similarly, pay attention to when your rental starts. If you rent at noon on one day and return the car at 1 p.m. the next, you'll pay for part of a second day. It might be worth arriving early at the airport in order to return the car in time to avoid paying for extra rental hours.

TIPPING

*A little extra cash is part of the cost
of services and travel.*

MAP IT

When you pay for a meal or a haircut, you may think it costs enough already. But the prices for many kinds of services are set below what they should be because a tip for the wait staff, cab driver, or stylist is an expected part of the total cost. Build tips into your budget for restaurant meals, cabs, haircuts, and certain services when you travel.

DIRECTIONS

You can—and should—tip more for outstanding service and a little less for wretched service. But you shouldn't stiff the provider if the service isn't to your liking. Tipping is part of the person's wages and also part of your costs.

Before you add on the tip, check your bill to be sure service isn't already included. Room service, for instance, often includes a charge for gratuity, and restaurants will often add 15 percent or more for groups of six or larger.

The nicest way to give a tip is with a smile and a thank-you. If you truly find that awkward, you can often leave a tip at the front desk of a hair salon, hotel, or spa.

THE DIRECT ROUTE

What to tip can be confusing. Below is a rule of thumb, though the custom may vary in your region. Ask friends, neighbors, and coworkers for guidance.

➤ **Wait staff at restaurants:** 15 percent, before sales tax, or 20 percent for very good service

➤ **Food-delivery people:** at least $1 or $2, or 10 percent of the total cost—tip more if the weather is unusually bad or it's a busy day, like Super Bowl Sunday

➤ **Takeout/coffee bars/other quick-service outlets:** You aren't required to tip. Unlike wait staff, these employees are paid minimum wage or better. But many of them rely on tips as a supplement to their fairly low income, and if you're a regular, you may want to drop something extra in the jar.

➤ **Bartender:** 15 percent of the tab or about $1 a drink if you pay as you go

➤ **Coat check:** $1 per item

➤ **Parking attendant:** $1 to $2 a car, more if you drive a fancy car or are at a fancy venue

➤ **Washroom attendant:** 50¢ to $1

➤ **Cab driver:** 15 percent, rounding up to the nearest dollar. Up to 20 percent in New York City. Add $1 or $2 if the driver helps with bags.

➤ **Hair stylist or barber:** 15 to 20 percent; if the stylist is also the salon owner, you don't necessarily have to tip. Ask the receptionist what's customary.

➤ **Shampoo person:** $1 to $2

➤ **Massage or other spa service:** 15 to 20 percent

➤ **Hotel doorman:** $1 for hailing a cab

➤ **Bellman:** $1 to $2 a bag, more in high-end hotels

➤ **Hotel housekeeper:** $1 to $2 a night, left on the dresser or table, up to $5 per night for high-end hotels

➤ **Skycap at airport:** $1 to $2 per bag on top of the airline's charge for curbside service or luggage

ADDITIONAL DIRECTIONS

For people who provide services for you year-round, it's a good practice (and a nice thing) to thank them with a gift or extra money at the end of the year. You know the person best, but here are some guidelines for end-of-the-year giving:

➤ **Hair stylist:** if you're a regular, the cost of a regular session, a gift, or both

➤ **Cleaning person:** the cost of one visit

➤ **Newspaper delivery person:** $10 to $25

➤ **Building super:** $50 to $100, though it could be more or less in your area or if the super has done repairs for you or been particularly helpful. Ask around your building

➤ **Apartment doormen:** $25 to $100 each

➤ **Personal trainer:** a gift or an amount up to one session, depending on how often you use the service and your relationship with the trainer

➤ **Doctor's-office staff:** candy, nuts, or food if you see the office staff regularly or if they've been particularly helpful

➤ **Mail carrier:** food or candy or small gift card. Rules prohibit gifts of more than $20 in value.

Scoring Tickets

Enjoying the good life within your budget.

MAP IT

Taking in a good play, hearing a favorite band, or strolling through the latest museum exhibit can cost a fortune, particularly in a big city. The fun stuff can seem out of reach if you're already on a very tight budget. But there's hope: There are cheaper options, especially if you're clever, patient, and determined.

DIRECTIONS

Like so many other products, tickets have hidden costs. Nearly all event sellers will tack on service charges, which can range from a dollar or two to more than 15 percent of the ticket cost. Some even charge to send tickets electronically rather than through the mail.

In most cases, you'll need a credit card to buy tickets, but some venues may only accept cash. If a show or concert is especially popular, you may need to be ready to buy the moment that tickets go on sale. Try a multitasking, multimedia approach, calling and clicking online at the same time.

THE DIRECT ROUTE

Getting a deal on tickets falls into several categories:

➤ **Lucky.** If you're a student, many theaters, symphonies, movie houses, and other venues will offer special student rates or discounts. Some will sell students greatly discounted tickets if you show up about an hour before the show. If you're going out, don't leave home without your student ID—you never know what discounts it may bring. Some shows may even have lotteries for a chance to buy cheaper tickets, student or not.

Some employers and building concierges also negotiate free or discounted offers for workers. Check out employee and office-building newsletters and Web sites to see what might be available. Ticket resale Web sites like www.StubHub.com may also have good deals.

➤ **Patient.** Museums often have regular free or discounted hours, though you may have to work your schedule around them.

Many theaters offer lower prices for matinees or less popular shows. They may also sell leftover tickets at deep discounts in the hour before the show starts.

TKTS in New York and similar ticket booths in other big cities sell theater tickets for a discount on the day of the show. Check the Internet for locations, to see what time you should show up, and if the booth takes credit cards or if it requires you to pay in cash.

Even sold-out concerts sometimes hold back a few tickets for people who show up the day of the performance. Showing up at the last minute may get you that coveted seat. And if you can wait until after the concert or ballgame starts, there's always a possibility that scalpers still holding tickets will sell them at a deep discount, just to recoup some of their investment.

➤ **Clever.** If your favorite band or group has a fan club or Web site fan list, sign up. Many performers will offer tickets to die-hard fans before they go on sale to the general public.

Watch for preview or dress-rehearsal performances, which may get you in at a reduced cost. Most cities also have all kinds of free events, from plays to book readings to concerts.

If you're fond of coupons, keep an eye out for discount books or passbook savings books sold by nonprofit organizations. These typically have dozens of coupons for discounted meals and various kinds of tickets.

For Broadway tickets, two groups in New York City, Theater Extras and Audience Extras, give away tickets to help theaters and others fill seats. You'll have to buy an annual membership at a cost of about $100 and pay small processing fees for your tickets. Once you're signed up, you can see what's available and request up to two tickets. In addition, www.BroadwayBox. com often has discounts on a wide range of New York plays and musicals.

For tickets that are truly in demand, keep an eye on the Web sites Stubhub and eBay, especially as the date gets closer. Many ticket brokers won't cut prices, but individuals who need to sell their tickets may be more flexible.

Get your friends together. A group of ten or more can usually arrange discounted group tickets to theater, music, art, and sporting events.

Consider volunteering or working as an usher at your favorite venue. The perks may be worth the work.

Gift Cards and Prepaid Cards

Free money that isn't always free.

MAP IT

Those retail gift cards and prepaid cards that you've gotten for birthdays and holidays can be a real boon, giving you free spending money. But some come with all kinds of strings attached. Retail cards may expire, or you may be assessed a fee for failing to use it within as little as a year. In addition, some troubled retailers have refused to honor their gift cards after they filed for bankruptcy-court protection. That means that fogetting about a card could be costly.

Prepaid cards, which may say Visa, MasterCard, or American Express on them, may require you to pay a fee every time you use them, eating into your gift. The same may be true for paychecks issued on prepaid cards, meaning someone else gets a bite of your cash.

DIRECTIONS

Read the fine print. Issuers of cards are required to tell you of any expiration dates and any fees. If the giver neglects to pass along the paperwork that goes with a card, you can ask for it or check the terms online at the issuer's Web site.

Many cards also include toll-free numbers that will give you your balance and may warn of key expiration dates or fees.

THE DIRECT ROUTE

If you aren't going to use the card soon after receiving it, these tips can help you get the most out of it:

➤ If you receive your paycheck on a prepaid card, it's time to open a free checking account at a convenient bank and sign up for direct deposit. There's no point in losing part of your paycheck to fees paid to someone who issues plastic cards.

➤ Keep your card in a place where you can get to it, and where you won't forget about it, in case you happen on a chance to use it. The cards in your desk drawer may never be used— and that's a lost opportunity.

➤ Write down the card number in a safe place, just in case the card is lost.

➤ If you aren't likely to use the card, consider swapping with a friend or family member or selling it to someone who'd rather have it. That's better than letting the money sit as a permanent loan to a big retailer.

GIVING TO CHARITY

*Good for the soul and
maybe for your taxes, too.*

MAP IT

Giving to a charitable organization can have all kinds of consequences—nearly all positive. Sure, it means spending money that doesn't go to food, rent, or retirement, but it also means helping a cause you care about. Giving is one of the ways your money and your spending become a reflection of your personal values.

If you're a homeowner, give away a lot of money, or otherwise have enough tax deductions to itemize them, you can take advantage of the tax break the government offers for charitable contributions. Otherwise, keeping track of your donations will help keep your spending priorities in line.

DIRECTIONS

Of course, you can give money to any organization you like. But since every group would love some of your hard-earned cash, you owe it to yourself to be selective.

It helps to pick organizations that you care about. You may also want to consider what kind of donor you want to be. You could split $100 into five different donations, or make a bigger splash with a single one.

You may also see a bigger impact donating to groups in your community than to national organizations. For instance, your area's Red Cross chapter or your local Multiple Sclerosis Society will put at least some of the money to work near your home, while donations to the national organization may be put to a different use, like covering national administrative costs.

You have a right to know how much of your gift goes to the group's work and how much goes to raising more money. If the organization or its Web site doesn't give you the details you are looking for, the Better Business Bureau's www.Give.org and www.CharityNavigator.org can help you learn more about what the group does and its financial strengths and weaknesses.

From a tax standpoint, only organizations that meet certain requirements as charities or religious groups, including educational institutions, museums, and theater groups, qualify for deductions. You can deduct cash donations to those groups, as well as contributions of clothes, household items, used cars, art, stock, or other goods. Used items, like last year's clothes, can be valued only at a garage sale or flea-market prices. More valuable items, like works of art, may require an appraisal. If your noncash contribution adds up to more than $500, you'll have to fill out an additional tax form.

You can't deduct donations to an individual, contributions to a political campaign or political group, raffle tickets, or the value of your time. If you buy a ticket to a dinner supporting a cause, you can only deduct the amount over and above the cost of the meal itself. If you join a museum and get free entrance to all exhibits, you can deduct only the value over the cost of your benefits. The museum will tell you what amount is deductible.

THE DIRECT ROUTE

For your own benefit, you should keep track of your donations. That will be much easier to do if you make all your donations with a check or credit card.

The IRS now requires some kind of receipt for every donation, no matter how small; stash your receipts in your tax file. (See "Paperwork," page 59.)

Some charities may have similar names but different standards and goals. For instance, the Juvenile Diabetes Research Foundation, the Diabetes Research and Wellness Foundation, and the Diabetes Action Research and Education Foundation, as well as the American Diabetes Association, all seek to find a cure for diabetes. Check the charity's Web site or its record on one of the charity sites mentioned above to be sure your donation goes to the group you want to support.

In addition, be skeptical of groups that sprout up after a big disaster, as many people learned after Hurricane Katrina. You can check out legitimate ones on the charity Web sites. Also avoid charities that give you a hard sell or want your check right away. Some of those may be spending more on fundraising than the charity itself.

Once you give to a charity or two, you may find your mailbox full of solicitations. Some charities may send you stickers or greeting cards in hopes that you'll feel guilty and respond. It's a ploy, and you don't owe them anything.

To end mailbox clutter, be sure to check the box on the charity's form that asks it to refrain from sharing your information. The Direct Marketing Association also offers options for cutting down unsolicited junk mail at www.DMAchoice.org.

If you give away a few thousand dollars a year, you may not have a big enough amount to itemize your deductions. One possible solution is to make all your donations every other year. That may give you a total big enough to deduct your charitable giving from your taxes.

ADDITIONAL DIRECTIONS

For information on charities that interest you, start with the charity's Web site. For additional information, check out www.Give.org, www.CharityNavigator.org, and www.Guide Star.org.

PART V

INVESTING IT

So far, this book has focused on ways to manage your money that comes in and goes out. This part aims to move your finances to a new level by helping you ensure a better future. Ultimately, investing is about getting ahead.

Unless you win the lottery or score a big inheritance, investing for the long term is your best shot at building the kind of wealth that will give you financial freedom down the road. How much you need to get there will depend entirely on your needs, wants, and spending style. But getting there at all will depend heavily on your discipline and determination in saving and investing your money now.

The biggest challenge in investing—other than saving—is sorting through the blizzard of often-conflicting advice and advisers to find methods that work best for you. Think of investing as something like fashion. If you found yourself with a completely empty closet, you might start with some basics—maybe some jeans and shirts. Then you would add your own style—flashy or conservative, dressy or dressed down, accessorized or plain vanilla.

We'll take the same approach here, starting with the basics and adding options to help you develop your own investing style.

Beginning to Invest

Some initial steps for your first foray into the market.

MAP IT

Perhaps the hardest aspect of investing is staying focused on your goals. The constant swarm of investing information—coming at you from television, magazines, bookshelves, and your friends and family—is that you have to win, you have to beat "the market" or some other intangible competitor. Worse, those pushing this advice imply that you need to win right away.

The reality is that investing is a long-term process. The money you put into stocks and bonds needs to be money that you won't need for some years—or maybe decades. Money that you need in the next three years should be in safer money-market or savings accounts.

Over that long time period, it *is* nice to beat the market, but it isn't crucial. What's really important is that you beat inflation, that nasty, nagging creep in everyday prices that means today's dollar will buy less tomorrow. If your investment returns over time beat inflation by a decent amount, you'll be ahead of the game.

Sure, the better your returns, the quicker you'll meet your financial goals. But stretching for far bigger and faster gains almost always means taking more risk—and that could mean much, much bigger losses in the periodic downturns that are part of any market. Those downturns can be brutal, as they were in fall 2008, when stocks plunged about 25 percent in a few weeks.

Just as you would build a wardrobe with the basics of pants and shirts, you build an investment portfolio with some simple building blocks. A sure-and-steady approach may not allow for a lot of boasting or make for spicy cocktail-party chatter. But in this race, it's a winning strategy, and essential for beginners.

DIRECTIONS

In the following chapters, we'll describe different kinds of investments in more depth. But here's what you need to know to get started: mutual funds. Especially index mutual funds.

Mutual funds are pools of money that invest in a number of stocks or bonds or a combination of the two. Index mutual funds seek to mimic the return of a specific basket of stocks or bonds, like the Standard & Poor's 500 Stock Index, which is made up of the stocks of 500 large and well-known companies.

Your very first long-term investment should be in a mutual fund that reflects the broad stock market because over time, the broad stock market has handily beaten inflation. The best options are an S&P 500 fund or a *total stock market fund,* which may invest in as many as 5,000 stocks.

That sounds simple enough, but finding affordable funds can be tricky. You can save money by being a do-it-yourself investor and avoiding funds that come with sales charges, or *loads,* that compensate stockbrokers and other sellers. You need to look for what's called a *no-load fund.* Many mutual funds now require a minimum initial investment of $2,500 to $3,000 and future investments of at least $100, although a few have minimums as low as $500. You may also be able to open an account by agreeing to invest a certain amount each month, usually $100, but occasionally $50.

You can invest directly with a mutual fund family or buy many no-load funds without added charges through fund supermarkets, such as discount broker Charles Schwab or the brokerage unit of Fidelity Investments. Schwab also offers a line of its own index funds with low minimum initial investments and reasonable expenses. Many other funds with low minimum investments, however, have very high expenses. You are better off waiting until you can make a larger initial investment. T. Rowe Price (minimum $2,500), Vanguard (minimum $3,000), and Fidelity are known for their low-cost, high-quality funds. For more details, see "Mutual Funds" on page 244.

To get around the minimum investment another way, you may also want to consider an exchange-traded fund that mimics the S&P 500 or a total market index fund. ETFs don't have a minimum investment, but have other features that can add to your costs (see "Exchange-Traded Funds," page 251).

If your first investment is a 401(k), refresh your memory with that chapter, page 90. As mentioned, your 401(k) will offer a select number of investment options, but that list will almost certainly include an S&P 500 or a total stock market fund or both. Those don't require a minimum initial investment, and because you can allocate your money in pieces in a 401(k)— even if it's just a few dollars a month—you can start to build a portfolio right away.

By the time you have $5,000 socked away for retirement or in long-term savings, you want to start diversifying, or building a portfolio of three to six different investments. Diversity should reduce your risk because when one area of the investing world is doing poorly, another usually is doing very well. (That isn't always true, however.)

Some investment professionals recommend that people in their twenties and thirties keep all of their retirement money in stocks, even though stocks can decline sharply, in some years dropping 40 percent or more. The rationale is that retirement is so far away that young people will have many years to make up any declines in stock values. Even so, a falling stock market can be frightening, and a portfolio that is invested only in stocks is best for risk-takers who can stomach watching their investments swiftly decline in value.

Many young investors will probably sleep better with at least 10 percent to 20 percent of their money in bonds. Funds that invest in inflation-protected U.S. Treasury securities, total-bond-market funds, or an intermediate-term bond fund make the best choices here. (For more information, see "Bonds," page 237.)

After that, you may want to further diversify your stock holdings by investing in an international stock index fund, a small-company fund, a real-estate investment trust fund, or some combination of the three.

With some combination of three or more of these funds, you'll have a pretty good wardrobe of investments that should meet most, if not all, of your needs.

THE DIRECT ROUTE

Brace yourself. Investing in stocks and bonds can be a hair-raising rollercoaster ride.

Some years, you will lose money. Other years, you will enjoy returns of more than 20 percent. This is how investing works. Over time, it should all pay off by beating inflation and giving you a genuine nest egg.

If you are investing for retirement or something many years away, whether it's in a 401(k), another retirement fund, or in long-term savings and you want an easy solution, there's a really simple shortcut. Look for a "balanced fund" or a "fund of funds" for a regular account. Vanguard's STAR Fund, for instance, invests in a mix of index funds and is intended to give you an instant diversified portfolio. While most Vanguard funds require a $3,000 initial minimum investment, the STAR Fund can be opened with $1,000.

For a retirement account or 401(k), look for a "target" or "life cycle" fund. These funds are managed with your retirement dates in mind, investing in stocks aggressively in the early years and becoming less aggressive later on. If you're twenty-five years old, you would pick a fund aimed at roughly 2050, or a thirty-five- to forty-year investment window. Put your money in that fund and check once or twice a year on a financial Web site to see how it's doing relative to its peers. You may not get record-setting results, but over time, your money should grow in the right direction.

If you want more control over your investments, you can try other mixes. Scott Burns, the long-time syndicated financial columnist, has famously touted "Couch Potato" investment portfolios that reduce risk while producing fine returns. His latest Couch Potato version calls for you to put half your money in a total stock market index fund and half in an inflation-protected securities fund. Once or twice a year, *rebalance*—that is, transfer funds from one to the other so that the ratio is 50-50 again. The rest of the year, he says, you can do something— anything—else other than think about your investments.

Burns also offers a variation, the Margaritaville Portfolio: one-third in a total stock market index fund, one-third in an inflation-protected securities fund, and one-third in a total international stock fund. That portfolio has consistently beaten the S&P 500.

You can also fashion your own mix, with 10 to 20 percent in an international fund, 5 to 10 percent in a real-estate investment trust fund, 5 to 10 percent or so in a small-company fund, 10 to 20 percent in a bond fund, and roughly half in a broad stock market fund. (For more on how to pick good funds, see "Mutual Funds" on page 244.)

You will probably fare better if you keep your investments simple and if you pick a course and stick with it. There is no perfect or "right" investment portfolio. No one will have your exact wardrobe, or make your exact financial choices.

SIMPLE INVESTING STRATEGIES

A few guidelines to keep you on track.

MAP IT

As you start to build your financial wardrobe, moving beyond a single mutual fund and figuring out your particular style, you will no doubt have lots of questions. Finding good advice in investing is especially difficult because everyone wants some of your hard-earned money.

Brokerage firms want you to generate commissions and fees, mutual-fund firms want you to add to their coffers, gurus want to sell books, and advisers want to send their kids to college and enjoy retirement just as much as you do.

Even financial planners who charge by the hour—the professionals who are most likely to offer unfettered advice tailored to your situation—will probably cost a minimum of $1,000 for their services. So until you have a decent-sized portfolio, you are more or less on your own, with the help of these guideposts.

DIRECTIONS: MAKING INVESTMENTS

Nowadays, you can buy stocks, bonds, and mutual funds almost anywhere—at a full-service firm such as Smith Barney; online through a discount brokerage such as Charles Schwab or TD Ameritrade; directly from an investment and mutual fund firm, such as Fidelity or T. Rowe Price; or even from the grocery store outlet of some banks.

The costs and the services you get will also vary widely. Full-service firms have their own research analysts and economists who study individual investments and the broader economy and markets. You will work directly with a specialist who can give you advice, explain different kinds of possibilities, and work with you to meet your goals. Since that specialist wants to make a living, you'll also pay commissions on most purchases or sales.

If you have enough money, you can also turn the whole process over to a money manager who will invest it for you for an annual fee of 1 percent or 2 percent of your portfolio. This is a costly way to go, since your return needs to be even better to cover your extra costs. Generally, you'll need at least $100,000 in investments, but more like $500,000 or $1 million, to make this kind of service worthwhile.

With a discount brokerage, by contrast, you'll have far less personal service. Most of your business will be online, or maybe by phone, but you will also pay far less for buying and selling.

Mutual fund companies including Fidelity, Vanguard, T. Rowe Price, and dozens of others will help you buy and sell the mutual funds they manage, often without any sales charge, and may also offer you a discount brokerage account for buying and selling individual stocks or bonds or other firms' mutual funds. For the most part, they'll make their money on the fees and expenses that your mutual funds pay as well as on commissions from other transactions.

THE DIRECT ROUTE FOR MAKING INVESTMENTS

You want to keep as much of your money as you can, so for now, you're better off going directly to a mutual fund company or using a discount broker. In addition to comparing costs, take a look at their Web sites and see if they are helpful and thorough in providing information, navigating you through the selection and purchasing process, and offering practical advice instead of a hard sell.

For advice and insight, you should pick your favorite financial Web sites. A number of financial Web sites, including WSJ.com, Morningstar, MarketWatch, Smart Money, Yahoo! Finance, and Kiplinger have sections that can help you suss out good, low-cost mutual funds and other investments.

DIRECTIONS: BUYING AND SELLING

It's worth repeating: Investing is a long-term process.

People who jump in and out of investments are gamblers, not investors.

Likewise, it is impossible to pick the perfect time to buy or sell. Sometimes we make the right call at the right time and see quick profits. But far more often than not, investing takes persistence and patience before you see a real payoff.

You should buy an investment because you have solid, practical reasons why you believe it should be worth more in the future than it is today. You should hold on to that investment as long as those reasons are true. When those reasons are no longer true or when you have a much better investment to make with that money, it's time to sell.

In other words, ignore whether an investment price is at a high or a low when you buy. What you want to assess is whether you think it will climb enough from today's price to make it a worthwhile use of your money.

Similarly, price itself is not a reason to sell. Some people sell because an investment has lost money. But if the reasons you bought it are still valid, a lower price may be a great time to buy more, not to sell.

At the other end of the spectrum, some people refuse to sell their losers because they feel like they should wait until they can get their money back. (In fact, that may never happen.) If you don't see prospects for a turnaround, sell and take the loss. Your money will work harder for you somewhere else.

Income taxes also come into play here. If you have owned the investment less than a year, you will pay taxes on any gains as if the profits were regular income. Capital gains on investments that you have held at least one year are currently taxed at a maximum rate of 15 percent.

If you have a big winner and are worried about the taxes, consider whether there's a loser you can dump to help offset what you will owe the IRS.

THE DIRECT ROUTE FOR BUYING AND SELLING

When markets turn against you, don't panic. True, a downturn can be very scary, especially if the decline is sharp and quick. But as an investor, you want to buy low and sell high, not the other way around. If the investment is a good one, it will eventually rebound.

Resist the urge to chase hot investments. Often the hottest investments have already turned in big gains and most of the juice is gone. You'll end up buying high and being disappointed.

You should also be skeptical of people promising quick returns or easy ways to make a buck. It's a terrible (but true) cliché, so let's say it only once: If it sounds too good to be true, it probably is.

One way to avoid worrying about the price you're paying—and to cut your risk—is to invest a fixed amount either every month or every quarter so that you buy at high prices, at low prices, and at prices in between. This regular investment strategy is called dollar-cost averaging and is a great way to build a nest egg in mutual funds. When you invest in your 401(k) every paycheck, you are automatically dollar-cost averaging. Many mutual fund companies will help you set up automatic monthly transfers of $100 or more from your checking account into a mutual fund, making dollar-cost averaging simple to do.

MAP: HOW DOLLAR-COST AVERAGING WORKS

Assume you invested $300 each quarter in an S&P 500 fund:

Period	Amount invested	Share price	Shares bought
March 31, 2005	$300	$108.79	2.76
June 30, 2005	$300	$109.81	2.73
Sept. 30, 2005	$300	$113.20	2.65
Dec. 30, 2005	$300	$114.92	2.61
March 31, 2006	$300	$119.24	2.52
June 30, 2006	$300	$116.99	2.56
Sept. 29, 2006	$300	$123.04	2.44
Dec. 29, 2006	$300	$130.59	2.30
March 30, 2007	$300	$130.83	2.29
June 29, 2007	$300	$138.43	2.17
Sept. 28, 2007	$300	$140.61	2.13
Dec. 31, 2007	$300	$135.15	2.22
March 31, 2008	$300	$121.75	2.46
	Total $3,900		31.84

The average share price paid of $122.48 is higher than the lowest price, but far lower than the peak in September 2007. In this way, dollar-cost averaging smooths out your investment costs.

In all your investments, stay the course. Buy-and-hold investors who stay on top of their stocks' performances and likely prospects for the future fare better in the long run than those who constantly jump from idea to idea or strategy to strategy.

DIRECTIONS: DIVERSIFICATION

Investing in a variety of opportunities will lower your risk and should, over time, give you better returns.

The professionals call this asset allocation and recommend that you invest in a mix of stocks, bonds, and cash, then diversify within those categories by purchasing different kinds of stocks and bonds.

As explained in the previous chapter, and as you'll see in more detail in the following chapters, stocks come in many flavors: international and domestic; stocks of small, medium, and large companies; stocks in companies that are growing at race-car speeds and in those that have fallen out of favor; and stocks that focus on real estate or technology or other niche sectors.

For the most part, stocks are riskier than bonds. When you're young and you have a long investing horizon, you can bet more heavily on stocks and take a bit more risk—for instance, by putting your money in fast-growing companies. As you age, and as you get closer to actually needing your savings, you'll want to make moves to conserve your gains by gradually moving to more stable investments like cash and bonds.

There are nifty asset allocation models online to help you figure it out, like this one from the Iowa Public Employees' Retirement System: www.IPERS.org/calcs/AssetAllocator.html. Each model will make different assumptions about important factors, like your tolerance for risk. Ultimately, the decision will be up to you.

THE DIRECT ROUTE FOR DIVERSIFICATION

Once or twice a year, you should review your asset allocation to see if you want to tweak your mix, but you should hold back the urge to simply jump to the sector that is doing the best.

Instead, you should rebalance, or move your money around until you're back at the same percentage mix of domestic stocks, international stocks, bonds, and cash as where you started that year.

That can be a difficult process to swallow and to follow through on. After all, you are selling your winners and adding to your losers. But this year's loser can easily be next year's winner—and you'll still own the current winners as well. Rebalancing regularly puts you in a better position to benefit no matter which way the various sectors go.

ADDITIONAL DIRECTIONS

The U.S. Securities and Exchange Commission has a wealth of information to help investors on its site, www.SEC.gov/investor/pubs.shtml.

The Wall Street Journal, newspaper business sections, and their Web sites, like WSJ.com, are also an excellent source of information about investing and money management.

STOCKS

Owning a piece of the action.

MAP IT

Stocks, also known as equities, represent ownership in a company. If you own even a single share, you are a part owner of that business. As a stockholder, you benefit from the profits a company makes. And in the long run, the more profit a company makes, the higher the stock price will go—and the more money you'll make.

On the flip side, companies with declining profits will, over time, have declining stock prices.

Ideas and theories about how to buy good stocks and put together lucrative stock portfolios fill shelves and shelves at libraries and bookstores. Most people don't have the time for that kind of research and are best served by purchasing mutual funds based on indexes or where professionals do the stock-picking. But understanding the various ways people look at stocks and value them will help you to select more attractive mutual funds for your portfolio.

DIRECTIONS

Companies sell stock to the public to raise money to fund their growth or to finance new projects. Each stock is identified by

READING A STOCK QUOTE

Microsoft Corp. (MSFT)   NASDAQ

Comprehensive Quote: 08/25/08 04:00 PM EDT

Last	Change	% Change	Volume
27.66	-0.18	-0.65%	51,381,730

Open	High	Low	Prior Day's Volume
27.61	27.84	27.46	47,930,392

52-Week High	52-Week Low	Prior Day's Close
37.50	23.19	27.84
(11/02/2007)	(07/01/2008)	

Snapshot quotes reflect real-time trades reported through Nasdaq only; comprehensive quotes reflect trading in all markets and are delayed at least 15 minutes. Volume updates from 4:00 a.m. - 8:00 p.m. ET.(More Info)

Other Prices

Hong Kong Germany Xetra • MORE

Historical Quotes

Closing prices since 1/2/1970.

date: [   ] [Go]

Stock Data

Market Cap(Mil)	254,187.40
P/E Ratio	14.89
Dividend Yield	1.58%
Latest Dividend	$0.11
Pay Date of Latest Dividend	09/11/08
Last Stock Split	100% stock div.
Date of Last Split	02/18/03
Shares Outstanding (Mil)	9,130.29
Public Float (Mil)	7,869.70

All data updated daily before market opens
Source: www.WSJ.com; copyright © 2008 by Dow Jones & Co.

1. The closing price
2. The change from the day before
3. The number of shares traded
4. The company's stock-market value today, calculated by multiplying the shares outstanding by the stock price
5. Price-to-earnings ratio, the stock price divided by the earnings per share over the last four quarters

6. A measure of the income from the stock. The dividend yield is calculated by dividing the dividends paid over the last four quarters by the stock price
7. The number of shares that can be traded by the public. The public float excludes shares held by company founders, executives or other insiders.

its one- to four-letter ticker symbol, a shorthand moniker for the company's name, like AAPL for Apple Computer and LUV for Southwest Airlines, representing its base at Dallas' Love Field airport.

A company's first public stock sale is called an initial public offering, or IPO. Once sold, the shares can be traded between investors, just like baseball cards. Owning individual stocks gives you the right to vote for company directors and on other issues at annual shareholders' meetings.

Companies can buy back their stock by making an offer directly to shareholders or by buying the shares in the stock market just like other investors, but stocks don't ever "come due" or expire.

Stocks are traded most working days on stock exchanges, giant financial marketplaces where buyers and sellers come together. The world's most prestigious is the New York Stock Exchange. The Nasdaq Stock Market is actually the biggest by volume and is best known as the home of many technology stocks.

With the advent of electronic trading, a company's shares can be traded at almost any minute, making them extremely *liquid*—or easy to buy or sell. (Other kinds of investments, like real estate, rare postage stamps, or precious artwork, may also be lucrative, but they are illiquid, or hard to cash in quickly.) The price of a heavily traded stock can change every few seconds based on supply and demand as buyers and sellers come together.

Because the stock market is in near-constant motion, politicians, government officials, business people, employees, and investors watch it for signs of how businesses are faring and how the general economy is doing. A *bull market* is one that is rising pretty consistently; a *bear market* is one in a fairly steep slide.

Lots of things can affect stock prices: consumer confidence, world events, interest rates, and the successes or troubles of individual companies and their competitors. Problems in one part of the stock market, like the credit crisis in 2008, can affect other sectors of stocks, too. Sometimes, investors are just in a good mood—or a foul one.

Since it's nearly impossible to generalize about every stock that is traded, *the market* usually means the performance of a few indexes. The Dow Jones Industrial Average, or just the Dow, is made up of thirty very large, well-known stocks and is often treated as the representative for the whole market.

Some people also follow the Standard & Poor's 500 Stock Index of large-company stocks, the technology-heavy Nasdaq 100, or the Russell 2000 index of small-company stocks. The Wilshire 4500 Index reflects nearly all the stocks traded in the United States except those in the S&P 500.

Investors tend to break stocks into different categories based on size and potential.

Rather than measuring, say, sales or profits, a company's stock is measured by its market value, or *market capitalization,* the number of shares the company has outstanding multiplied by its current stock price. Companies with a market value of $10 billion or more have *large-cap* stocks. Companies with a market value of roughly $2 billion to $10 billion are considered *midcap* stocks. And companies with a value of about $300 million to $2 billion are *small caps.*

Those valued at a mere $300 million or less? *Micro caps.*

Investors also zero in on whether a company shares some of its profits by paying a quarterly dividend, a cash payment to shareholders. And they look at how much profit the company earns for each share that has been issued, a number known as earnings per share.

Then, to see how the stock market values one company relative to another, investors turn to the equivalent of a stock's SAT score: the price-to-earnings, or P/E, ratio. The ratio—the current stock price divided by the earnings per share over the last twelve months—tells you how much investors are willing to pay for every dollar that a company earns.

Most years, stocks have an average P/E ratio of 15 to 20, meaning investors are willing to pay $15 to $20 for each dollar of profits. But growth stocks, shares of companies that are growing much faster than average, tend to have P/E ratios of 30 or more. That means investors will pay far more for each $1 of earnings because they believe the company's expansion will pay off later in a much higher stock price.

By contrast, value stocks are the underappreciated underdogs in the market and may have single-digit P/E ratios. They may be in industries that are out of favor, or a company that has hit a rough spot but is expected to fix its problems. Investors buy these because they believe the market has undervalued them. Warren Buffett, one of the world's best-known and most successful investors, made his billions by seeking out value stocks.

Occasionally, a stock is both a growth stock and a value stock—growing quickly but with a stock price that some think is still below its true worth.

THE DIRECT ROUTE

Once you understand the different kinds of stocks, it's easier to figure out what mix of growth or value mutual funds and small- or large-cap stocks you want to own. The most diversified portfolios contain a mix of U.S. and international stocks, growth and value stocks, and stocks of different-sized companies.

In addition, once you've built a mutual fund portfolio, you may want to dabble in a few individual stocks to further round out your holdings (though you certainly don't need to). In particular, you should look for local or regional success stories that you can invest in early, before the company is famous enough for big mutual funds to find it.

Investment clubs, where members contribute a fixed dollar amount each month and take turns studying companies, are a good way to get experience researching, buying, and selling stocks.

Every time you buy or sell a stock, you will pay a sales commission. If you use an online broker, that commission may be

$10 or less—but it's still a cost of the investment. Trading frequently will run up your costs and reduce your return.

If you prefer to own individual stocks instead of mutual funds, you need to own more than one or two to reduce your risk and diversify your holdings. Just as you wouldn't want a fantasy baseball team of just pitchers and catchers, you need to own at least ten stocks in different industries with different characteristics.

Doing that requires a fair bit of research and homework. Avoid taking tips at face value from television, the Internet, magazines, or mailings. Instead, you need to study the company's current financial situation and its future financial prospects, as well as the quality of its business and its management, subjects that are covered in business publications like *The Wall Street Journal.*

ADDITIONAL DIRECTIONS

For more information on stocks, see *The Wall Street Journal. Complete Money and Investing Guidebook* or *The Wall Street Journal. Complete Personal Finance Guidebook.* Classic investing books include Benjamin Graham's *The Intelligent Investor,* William Bernstein's *The Four Pillars of Investing,* Burton G. Malkiel's *A Random Walk Down Wall Street,* and Philip A. Fisher's *Common Stocks and Uncommon Profits and Other Writings.*

BONDS

Investing in other people's debt.

MAP IT

Bonds are a form of debt. When a company or government issues bonds, it promises to pay interest on the debt and to repay the debt on a specific date.

The U.S. Treasury sells bonds to finance the federal government. Schools and cities sell them to help build new buildings, and companies issue them to help fund their new projects and operations.

People buy bonds for the interest income they pay, which is often higher than what you'd get for a savings account or a money-market fund. Retired people and nervous investors like them because they pay a fixed amount of cash interest, usually twice a year. For that reason, bonds are also known as *fixed-income* securities.

People also own bonds because they reduce the overall riskiness of their portfolios. Because investors expect bonds to be repaid or redeemed at their date of *maturity,* they are considered safer than stocks, which are never "repaid." But repayment usually isn't guaranteed, and bonds can be risky if a company or government defaults, or can't pay its debt. Understanding those risks can help you sort out when you want to invest in bonds and how you want to do it.

(*Bonds,* by the way, is a catch-all term, but especially applies to debt that is issued for ten years or more. Short- to medium-term loans up to ten years in duration are also often called *notes.* Treasuries that are shorter than a year are known as *bills.*)

DIRECTIONS

Bonds are all about the interest, or income, they generate. In 2007, Starbucks sold $550 million in ten-year debt to investors. The debt pays an interest rate of 6.25 percent, which is also known as the coupon. (In fact, once upon a time, bonds came with coupons, which investors clipped twice a year to collect their interest.) The repayment date, August 2017, is also known as the maturity date.

If you bought a $1,000 Starbucks bond when it was issued and held it until it was repaid, you would receive interest payments twice a year totaling $62.50. Then on the maturity date, you would get your $1,000 back. Simple enough.

During the time you owned your bond, however, the price of it would fluctuate up and down depending on interest rates and the prices buyers and sellers were willing to pay. Bond prices and interest rates move in inverse directions, with bond prices rising as interest rates fall, and vice versa. Why? Because when interest rates go up in the economy, people want more income from a bond investment, so they aren't willing to pay as much for the bond itself. Conversely, when interest rates fall, people are willing to pay a premium for a bond that pays a better interest rate.

If that's confusing, don't worry. Here's what you really need to know: Just like stocks, bond prices can rise and fall on any given day. The closer the bond gets to its maturity date, the more likely it is to be close to its original, or *par,* value, usually $1,000.

The quality of the borrower, or *issuer,* can also affect a

bond's riskiness. Just as a credit score gives clues as to whether you may have trouble repaying your debt, credit ratings tell you about the quality of corporate and government bonds. Standard & Poor's and Moody's are the two biggest credit rating companies. The table below shows how they grade bonds and bond quality. The Starbucks bond was rated BBB+ by Standard & Poor's and Baa1 (with the "1" equivalent to a "+") by Moody's, giving it a good grade, but not a great one. Bonds rated BB or Ba and lower are considered speculative, or *junk*, bonds. While most bonds are repaid as expected, junk bonds are considered riskier than investment-grade bonds. Investors demand higher interest rates on junk bonds because they have a greater risk of default.

MAP: BOND RATINGS

Standard & Poor's	Moody's	
AAA	Aaa	Best quality
AA	Aa	
A	A	
BBB	Baa	
BB	Ba	"Junk bonds"
B	B	
CCC	Caa	
CC	Ca	
D	C	In default

Bonds are sometimes classified as senior or subordinated debt depending on where they fall in the companies' hierarchy of borrowing. If a company runs into serious trouble and ends up in bankruptcy court, its lenders are repaid based on their ranking. Not surprisingly, the IRS gets paid first. Banks usually get paid next, and then "senior" bondholders. Holders of subordinated bonds are next. The stock has value only if there is money left over after all the lenders are paid. Sometimes, the stockholders end up with nothing while bondholders get some or all of their money back—another reason bonds are considered a relatively safe investment.

If you buy a corporate bond and hold on to it, you'll pay tax only on the interest you receive. If you sell the bond at a profit, however, you'll also pay tax on the gain. By contrast, the interest paid on *municipal bonds,* those issued by state and local governments, are exempt from federal taxes and state taxes in the state where they are issued. They pay a lower interest rate than comparable corporate bonds to account for the difference in taxes.

THE DIRECT ROUTE

Remember how owning stock mutual funds is considered less risky than owning one stock because it gives you diversity? The picture for bonds is a little more complicated.

Investing in a bond mutual fund that owns many different corporate bonds means you have less risk of default than if you just owned one bond outright. And a fund may spread your dollars among different kinds of bonds—such as government, corporate, and mortgage-backed bonds—protecting you if one of those sectors runs into problems.

But bond funds don't mature, even though each bond is eventually repaid. Because bond prices can sink or surge when overall interest rates are climbing or falling, the value of a bond fund can swing sharply as well.

By contrast, when you own an individual bond, you can more easily ignore those ups and downs in price and hold your one bond until it matures.

Short-term bond funds are considered the least risky. Since a short-term bond may only have a year or two until its maturity, when investors will be repaid at par, the bond's price won't tumble too far below that level or rise too far above it. Long-term bond funds, or funds that invest in bonds that don't mature for many years, may pay a higher interest rate but are considered the riskiest because their prices can be fairly volatile.

As a result, many professionals recommend intermediate-term bond funds, those investing in bonds that mature in two to seven years. Those are likely to pay a higher interest rate than short-term funds but they should be somewhat more stable than long-term bond funds.

If you want regular income from your investments, you may want to buy individual bonds that will pay you interest regularly. You can build a bond *ladder*, buying bonds that mature in two years, four years, six years, and so on. When the first bond matures, you replace it with, say, a bond that matures in eight years. That way, you consistently get the benefit of higher interest rates on longer-term bonds while taking less risk than investing only in long-term bonds.

You can buy U.S. Treasury bonds at www.TreasuryDirect. gov, with a minimum purchase of $100.

Buying and selling individual corporate bonds is much harder than buying and selling stocks. Many bonds trade only every few days. There are also fewer buyers and sellers, so it can be more difficult to know if you are getting a fair price. The most actively traded bonds are listed online in the market data section of WSJ.com or in the newspaper.

Many brokers, including Charles Schwab, now list their inventories of corporate bonds online, making bond buying simpler. A broker can also help you find bonds that meet your needs.

When you consider a bond, you should be most interested in the interest rate, or *yield*, you will receive relative to the risk you will take. Generally, you want a bond with a high Moody's and Standard & Poor's rating that pays a reasonable return

READING BOND PRICES

Most Active Investment Grade Bonds

Issuer Name	Symbol	Coupon	Maturity	Rating Moody's/S&P/ Fitch	High	Low	Last	Change	Yield %
		①	②	③	④	④	④	⑤	⑥
BOEING CAPITAL	BA.IM	6.500%	Feb 2012	A2/A+/A+	101.380	99.000	101.110	-0.290	6.119
AMBAC FINANCIAL GP	ABK.GH	5.950%	Dec 2035	A3/A/--	42.000	40.000	42.000	6.000	14.612
GOLDMAN SACHS GP	GS.YW	6.150%	Apr 2018	Aa3/AA-/AA-	87.125	79.030	86.450	4.056	8.245
GENERAL ELECTRIC CAPITAL CORP	GE.HCE	5.000%	Apr 2012	Aaa/AAA/--	96.337	91.667	93.100	-0.330	7.300
EMBARQ CORP	EQ.GC	6.738%	Jun 2013	Baa3/BBB-/BBB-	89.500	82.926	85.000	-1.423	10.985
JPMORGAN CHASE & CO	JPM.JPF	6.000%	Jan 2018	Aa2/AA-/AA-	93.130	89.891	90.472	-2.028	7.446
GENERAL ELECTRIC CAPITAL CORP	GE.HEH	5.875%	Jan 2038	Aaa/AAA/--	75.660	70.514	72.703	1.572	8.393
VIACOM	VIA.GL	7.700%	Jul 2010	Baa3/BBB/BBB	92.815	89.333	89.625	-0.375	14.609
GOLDMAN SACHS GP	GS.OU	5.700%	Sep 2012	Aa3/AA-/AA-	92.500	88.000	89.500	-0.985	8.992
AT&T	T.KF	6.300%	Jan 2038	A2/A/A	79.600	75.965	78.013	-1.587	8.313

Source: www.WSJ.com; copyright © 2008 by Dow Jones & Co.

1. The coupon is the interest paid annually on a bond. A holder of a $1,000 bond with a 6.40% coupon will receive $64 a year in interest.
2. "Maturity" is when the bond is to be repaid.
3. The rating measures how risky the investment is. The more "As," the more likely the bond is to be repaid. The lowest investment-grade bond rating is BBB (Standard & Poor's) or Baa (Moody's).
4. Bonds typically are issued in $1,000 increments, but their prices are reported without the last zero. So a bond with a price of 99.640 actually costs $996.40.
5. Change in price from the previous day's closing price.
6. Yield is the return the investor receives if the bond is bought today and held until maturity

relative to similar bonds. Because you may pay more or less than the par value, there are different kinds of yields. The *yield to maturity* is the interest rate you will receive if you buy the bond today, reinvest the interest you receive, and hold the bond until its final day.

Some bonds can be *called,* or repaid earlier than maturity. The *yield to call* is the interest rate you will receive between now and the call or early repayment date.

Municipal bonds make sense mostly if you are in a high tax bracket. If you are in a lower tax bracket, you'll probably earn more with corporate bonds, even after taxes.

ADDITIONAL DIRECTIONS

To understand more about bonds, go to www.SmartMoney.com/onebond. This site includes a calculator, when to buy bond funds, when to buy individual bonds, and a living *yield curve,* showing the current yields on bonds with different maturities.

MUTUAL FUNDS

The power in numbers.

MAP IT

Mutual funds help individuals invest like the professionals do. By pooling the investments of many people into one big mutual fund, fund managers can invest in far more stocks and buy and sell at a much lower cost than someone investing alone.

Funds may invest in stocks or bonds or a combination of the two. In fact, there are so many different possibilities that there are many more mutual funds to choose from than there are individual stocks.

Like stocks and bonds, mutual funds can climb or fall in value. They may also have additional fees and expenses that are apparent as well as some that are less visible. Understanding how mutual funds work is crucial to understanding your investments.

DIRECTIONS

While you can trade a stock or bond at almost any moment of the day, you can't trade mutual funds the same way. Because so many stocks or bonds may be moving at once during the trading day, mutual funds are priced and sold only once a day, at the close of regular stock trading.

That means you can buy or sell only at that day's price, and only after the markets have finished for the day. Since you're investing for the long term, it shouldn't matter. But in reality, it can be frustrating to finally decide on a fund and put in an order, only to see the market have a big rally before your purchase is made.

When you invest in a mutual fund, the share price you pay is based on the fund's *net asset value,* all of its assets divided by the number of shares outstanding.

Funds sold through brokers or financial advisors may include an upfront sales commission of 3 percent to 6 percent of your investment or a sales charge when you sell your holdings. This charge is called a load.

Funds that don't charge any of these commissions are *no-load* funds. Generally, no-load funds are preferred over load funds because you get to keep more of your money. But the rare load fund that has a superior performance year in and year out may more than make up for the additional cost when you initially invest.

To discourage active trading in and out of mutual funds, some funds have added redemption fees for those who haven't held the fund for very long. For instance, if you sell within ninety days of investing in a fund, you may be assessed a fee that will diminish any returns you have. If you're selling a fund that you've held less than a year, check to be sure you won't pay extra for the decision.

Funds also have operating fees and expenses that are deducted from the total assets—that is, before you actually see the fund's results. Higher expenses can eat away at your return, and make a significant dent in your fund's growth over time.

When you invest in a fund, you'll want to understand its strategy. Knowing the focus of your funds will help you diversify your portfolio and ensure that you don't own several funds that all own similar stocks.

For instance, is the mutual fund narrowly focused, like one that invests only in technology, or broad, like a fund that mimics the S&P 500 Stock Index? Is it a *balanced* fund that seeks to help you find the right mix of stocks and bonds? Is it actively managed by a group of professional stock pickers who are constantly buying and selling? Does it invest in small-, medium-, or large-cap companies, and are they mostly growth or value companies?

Map: A Mutual Fund "Style" Box

This chart, created by Morningstar, which provides research on mutual funds, helps define a fund's strategy in graphic terms.

STYLE		
Value	Blend	Growth

			Large	M
				A
			Medium	R K E T
				C A P
			Small	

Source: Copyright © 2008 by Morningstar, Inc. All rights reserved.

Mutual funds also have different tax consequences than stocks or bonds. As with those securities, if you sell a fund and the net asset value or NAV is higher than what you originally paid, you will pay tax on your profit. You will also owe taxes on dividends and interest the fund pays you. Here's the added wrinkle: When funds sell securities, they must distribute to shareholders most of the net capital gain they realize. Those gains are taxable to you—even though you didn't make a decision to sell anything. Once a year, you'll get a tax statement showing the portion that you will report on your taxes, which is hard to predict. Depending on the buying and selling that took place, it's entirely possible that you will pay capital gains taxes in a year when your mutual fund investments lost money. Still, paying those taxes now reduces what you have to pay if you sell your fund investment for a profit later.

THE DIRECT ROUTE

With so many different choices, picking a few funds for your portfolio can feel bewildering. Beyond the fund-selection suggestions in "Beginning to Invest" (page 219) and the ideas in "Simple Investing Strategies" (page 224), here are the key considerations when choosing funds:

Expenses. Any money that goes to the mutual fund company for running or advertising a fund is money that doesn't go to you. Even in a very basic choice like a Standard & Poor's 500 Stock Index fund, the expenses can vary widely. How much does it matter? Using Morningstar.com's "cost analyzer," we can look at the difference between investing in Vanguard's S&P 500 fund, which has annual expenses of $1.50 per $1,000 invested, and UBS S&P 500 fund C shares, which have annual expenses of $14.50 per $1,000 invested.

Let's assume we invested $1,000 in each and added $100 per month for twenty years. Hypothetically, let's also assume an annual return of 8 percent. After two decades, you'd have more than $60,000 in the Vanguard fund and you would have paid about $703 in expenses. But you would have just over $51,000 in the UBS fund and you would have paid more than $6,000 in expenses during the same time frame.

When you look up a fund, check out the expense ratio. Some Web sites will also show the average expense ratio in that category for comparison.

Loads. Many stockbrokers and financial advisers will direct you to funds that charge loads because they collect commissions or other income for those sales. Unless the performance of those funds is extraordinary, you should stick with no-load funds whenever possible.

Long-term Thinking. As you evaluate the types of funds you want in your portfolio, focus on both the long-term performance and the mix or diversification they provide. Since we'd all like to make money fast, it's tempting to chase whatever single fund is doing well right now. But those funds' successes may be temporary. Instead, look for funds that have performed better than average compared with similar funds for three years, five years, and even ten years.

True, this is investing based on past performance. That's dangerous because the past never accurately predicts the future. But a solid long-term performance through good years and bad ones is at least an indication that a fund is well managed and concentrating on the right things.

Most snapshots of mutual funds on financial Web sites will show you the fund's one-year, three-year, five-year, and ten-year performances. They should also show you how that compares to a benchmark index in the same category, like the S&P 500 for large stocks or the Russell 2000 for small stocks.

In addition, Morningstar and Lipper both rate funds based on performance, expenses, and other factors. While these assessments, too, are looking backward rather than forward, they can be useful tools in gauging how a fund compares with its competitors.

Other Factors. If you want to dig in and really research your funds, you should also consider the tenure and quality of the

UNDERSTANDING MUTUAL FUND PRICES

(3)

VANGUARD INDEX FUNDS: VANGUARD 500 INDEX FUND; INVESTOR SHARES   VFINX

(1) As of 8/22/08
NAV: 119.36   **(2)** 1-Day Net Change
▲ 1.35

1-Day Return
▲ 1.14%

YTD Total Return
▼ -10.82%

Category
S&P 500 Index   **(4)**

(5) LIPPER LEADER SCORECARD

(5) (5) (5) (4) (5)

Total Return   Consistent Return   Preservation   Tax Efficiency   Expense

LIPPER Higher (5) (4) (3) (2) (1) Lower

More on Lipper Leaders

TOTAL RETURNS (%) 3, 5 and 10 year returns are annualized.   **(6)**

	YTD	1Yr	3Yr	5Yr	10Yr
Fund	-10.82	-9.96	3.77	7.27	3.41
Category	-11.04	-10.33	3.35	6.85	3.03
Index (S&P 500)	-10.80	-9.90	3.90	7.40	3.50
% Rank in Category	14	17	16	16	7
Quintile Rank	A	A	A	A	A

FUND STATS

Portfolio Style:	S&P 500 Index
(7) Net Assets ($Mil):	54,221.10
Inception Date:	8/31/76
(8) Expense Ratio:	0.15%
Sales Charge:	
(9) Load Type	No Load
Front-End Load	0.00%
Back-End Load	0.00%

Investment Policy: The Fund seeks to track the performance of a benchmark index that measures the investment return of large-capitalization stocks. The Fund employs a "passive management" approach designed to track the performance of the Standard & Poor's 500 Index.

PURCHASE INFO

(11) Status to New Investors:	Open
Manager Name:	Michael H. Buek
Manager Start Date:	2000
Initial Purchase Regular:	$3,000
Phone Number:	800-662-7447

TOP 10 HOLDINGS (as of 3/31/08)   **(10)**

Name	% Net Assets
Exxon Mobil Corp	3.91
General Electric Co	3.19
At&t Inc	2.00
Microsoft Corp	1.96
Procter & Gamble Co	1.86
Johnson & Johnson	1.59
Chevron Corp	1.53
Bank Of America Corp	1.46
International Business Machines Corp	1.38
Jpmorgan Chase & Co	1.26

Source: www.WSJ.com; copyright © 2008 by Dow Jones & Co.

1. The NAV is the net asset value, or the assets divided by the number of shares. Mutual funds are bought and sold once a day, at the end of market trading, at the NAV price
2. The change since the previous trading date
3. How the fund has performed so far this year, or year-to-date
4. The category of fund, which could be an index fund, large cap, small cap, growth, value, domestic or international, among others
5. How the fund is ranked by Lipper, a major mutual-fund research firm
6. How the fund has performed over time, compared with its category, and compared with the index that serves as a benchmark. Fund results are usually shown for the year-to-date, one year, three years, five years, and 10 years. The three, five, and 10-year numbers are average annual returns. That is, the fund has averaged a 7.3% return over five years, but it may have been up quite a bit one of those years and down another
7. Net assets reflect how much money is invested in the fund
8. The expense ratio shows how much of the assets go to managing the fund. In this case, investors pay $1.50 in expenses for every $1,000 invested
9. Loads are additional charges paid when you buy or sell a fund's shares
10. These are the top stockholdings
11. Manager information and the minimum initial purchase

managers and how actively they are trading in and out of stocks. Generally, you want a manager with a proven track record in generating strong returns.

Information about fund managers and their experience should be available on the fund's Web site. *The Wall Street Journal* publishes a monthly mutual fund report. In addition, more detailed insight may be found on www.Morningstar.com, though it may require a paid membership to the site.

A fund's trading activity is measured by the turnover rate, or what percentage of stocks turn over every year. The higher the turnover rate, the more likely it is that managers are moving in and out of stocks quickly rather than holding for a longer term.

In addition, it can be helpful to look at a fund's top five to top ten holdings, information that is available on their Web sites or in reports mailed to your home. If you see that several of your funds are heavily invested in the same stocks, you might need to diversify a little better.

The Size of Your Investment. If you start out small, you may have to choose a fund with somewhat higher expenses. But as your nest egg grows to $10,000 or $50,000 or more, you should be able to switch to lower cost funds. For retirement accounts, the change should be tax free. Switching out of your regular accounts, however, may have tax consequences worth considering.

ADDITIONAL DIRECTIONS

For more on mutual funds, check out anything by John Bogle, the founder of Vanguard, such as *Common Sense on Mutual Funds* or *The Little Book of Common Sense Investing*. His followers are so devoted that they call themselves Bogleheads.

On www.Morningstar.com, the Vanguard Diehards forum is a highly regarded discussion of mutual fund and stock-market strategies.

Exchange-Traded Funds

Sort of a mutual fund,
sort of a stock.

MAP IT

Exchange-traded funds are a mixed breed: They trade on exchanges just like stocks, and can be bought or sold at any hour of the day from a brokerage account. But they are made up of baskets of stocks or bonds, just like mutual funds.

Many so-called ETFs mimic stock indexes like the S&P 500, the total stock market, or a bond index. Others focus on various sectors of the market, from health care to alternative energy to Swedish stocks.

Because ETFs don't require a minimum investment, they can be useful to fill in gaps in a portfolio or to help you get started. But they come with some quirks that make them somewhat less appealing than mutual funds, especially if you invest small sums on a regular basis.

DIRECTIONS

The biggest attraction of ETFs is their low expense ratio. The ETFs that track the S&P 500 Index, SPDRS (called Spiders) and iShares S&P 500, have annual expenses of 70¢ to $1 per $1,000 invested. That's as low as or lower than the very cheapest equivalent mutual funds, which require a minimum investment.

There's a hitch, of course: Because ETFs are traded like stocks, you must pay a commission each time you buy or sell. Even if your commission is just $10, you are still adding to the cost of owning the fund. If you trade in and out, your costs may more than outweigh the low expenses.

ETFs also have another appeal: lower taxes than equivalent mutual funds. Because of the way they are structured, you rarely have to pay capital gains taxes if you simply hold the ETF. Of course, if you sell an ETF at a profit, you will still pay taxes on any gains.

THE DIRECT ROUTE

If you intend to buy an index fund and hold on to it for while, ETFs could save you some money in taxes and expenses. But they are best suited for a single, one-time investment.

Avoid ETFs if you add regularly to your investment, if you dollar-cost average, or if you rebalance your portfolio regularly. Your commission costs will eat up too much of your savings.

You're also better off sticking with ETFs that mimic well-known indexes, like the major stock and bond indexes, or using them sparingly to dabble a little bit in a specific area you think might take off.

Still, you should research any fund before you jump in so that you know exactly what you're buying. Many of the raft

UNDERSTANDING EXCHANGE TRADED FUND PRICES:
Vanguard Total Stock Market Index, symbol: VTI

ETF SNAPSHOT

Sign up for Price & Volume Alerts

Vanguard T Stk Idx;ETF (VTI)
1:54 pm ET 8/28/08

Price: **$65.23**   Change: 0.80   % Change: 1.24%   Volume: **709,967**   52 Week High: **78.26**   52 Week Low: **60.00**

Performance (%) total return, cumulative through prior close.

	VTI	SP500
1 Day	0.88	0.37
1 Week	0.58	0.39
1 Year	-9.02	-12.70
3 Years	14.57	10.11
5 Years	47.14	36.51

VTI Daily —   © BigCharts 8/28/08

Compare to Index: Select
Period: 1D | 1W | 1M | 3M | 6M | 1Y | 3Y | 5Y Custom ▶
▶ Go to Interactive Charting

Note: Comparisons show price change only; not total return.

Investment Information

Market Cap	$10,306,287,230
Net Assets	$10,059,700,000
NAV	$64.53
Prem/Discount	-0.15%
Shares Outstanding	159,961,000
Avg Daily Vol	1,683,200
Dividend Yield %	1.94
Latest Dividend	$0.31 - 06/24/2008

The Fund seeks to track the performance of a benchmark index that measures the investment return of the overall stock market. The Fund employs a "passive management" approach designed to track the performance of the MSCI US Broad Market Index.

Dividend yield is based on regular and irregular dividends and may not reflect an established regular annual rate. Initial monthly and quarterly dividends are annualized and presented as an annual yield.

Detailed Information

Style	Core
Market Cap Classification	Multi-Cap
Asset Class	Equity
Inception Date	05/24/2001
Primary Exchange	AMEX
Mgmt Co	VANGUARD GROUP INC
Administrator	VANGUARD GROUP INC
Turnover	4.00
Beta	1.01
P/E	20.88
P/B	4.24
Expense Ratio	0.07

Top 10 Holdings

Company Name	% of Total Portfolio	Dollar Value (in thousands)
EXXON MOBIL CORP	3.24%	$325,934.28
GENERAL ELECTRIC CO	2.37%	$238,414.89
MICROSOFT CORP	1.87%	$188,116.39
AT&T INC	1.58%	$158,943.26
PROCTER & GAMBLE CO	1.43%	$143,853.71
CHEVRON CORP	1.24%	$124,740.28
JOHNSON & JOHNSON	1.20%	$120,716.40
BANK OF AMERICA CORP	1.14%	$114,680.58
APPLE INC	1.07%	$107,638.79
CISCO SYSTEMS INC	1.02%	$102,608.94
Total:	16.16%	$1,625,647.52

Source: www.WSJ.com; copyright © 2008 by Dow Jones & Co.

1. The current price, which will change during the trading day
2. The change in price from the close on the previous trading day
3. The number of shares traded today
4. How the ETF has performed over time compared with a benchmark index, the S&P 500. These returns are cumulative, or total, over time, not annual averages
5. General information similar to what you would see for both a stock and a mutual fund
6. The top 10 stock holdings underlying the ETF. These are similar to the S&P 500 holdings on p. 249.
7. The average price-to-earnings ratio for the stocks in the index
8. The expenses investors pay. In this case, investors pay 70¢ in expenses for every $1,000 invested

of new funds are so narrowly defined or so rarely traded that their prices can be very volatile. Some country-specific or industry-specific ETFs also have fairly high expenses. To check out the funds, look at investing Web sites or www.ETF connect.com. WSJ.com has an ETF screener in the market data part of its site.

RETIREMENT AND THE TAX MAN

Your investing-for-later options outside of work.

MAP IT

Much like your 401(k) options at work, there are two ways to beat the tax man with Individual Retirement Accounts: The traditional IRA lets you take a tax deduction now and pay taxes later, when you're a senior citizen and your tax rate might be lower. The other, the Roth IRA, requires you to pay taxes now but withdraw money tax free later on.

While pension plans and 401(k) plans are offered by employers, you set up and manage an IRA yourself. These retirement accounts can be particularly valuable for people whose retirement-savings options are limited—the self-employed, stay-at-home spouses, and those without access to better plans. If you are self-employed, for example, you may qualify to contribute to a SEP IRA, or a *simplified employee pension* plan. If you are covered by a plan at work, you may also be able to contribute to an IRA, depending on your income.

Before you figure you've heard enough about retirement and turn the page, consider this: The Roth IRA is also incredibly flexible, allowing you to take out the money you have contributed, without penalty, for any reason. Only the earnings on your money must stay in the account to avoid penalties and even those can be used for special circumstances, like a down payment on a first house. That means you can contribute to an account where your money can grow faster, but also have access to that money if you really need it.

If you are young, you may want to consider a Roth IRA if you have any employment income at all. You may also want to consider a traditional IRA if you work at a place that doesn't have a retirement plan or if your spouse works but you don't. Either way, your money can grow in these accounts without being taxed.

DIRECTIONS

To take advantage of either type of IRA, you either need income from a job or you must be a nonworking spouse. If you work and you earned more than $5,000, you could contribute up to $5,000 to either a traditional or Roth IRA or a combination in 2009, depending on other restrictions. If you earned less, you can contribute up to the amount of your compensation.

Let's start first with the Roth IRA. In 2009 you could open or add to one if you were single and your adjusted gross income for tax purposes was less than $120,000. If you were married and filing taxes together, your adjusted gross income must have been less than $176,000.

You cannot deduct contributions you make to a Roth IRA from your taxes; you can only make your investment with after-tax dollars.

The real payoff comes at retirement and beyond. Assuming you've had the account at least five years and can leave the money alone until you're 59½, any withdrawals you make will be tax free, regardless of whether they were contributions or earnings on your money. Income that isn't taxed, naturally, means more money for you later.

Beyond that, if you never touch the money, you can leave it to your heirs, tax free. That's about as nice a gift as you could give.

A traditional IRA works quite differently. In 2008, you could contribute up to $5,000 to a traditional IRA and deduct your contributions from your taxes if you didn't have another retirement plan.

If you were covered by another retirement plan, you could contribute (and deduct) up to $5,000 to a traditional IRA in 2009 if you were single and had an adjusted gross income of less than $65,000, or if you were married, filing taxes jointly, and had an adjusted income of less than $109,000 combined. If your spouse was covered by a retirement plan and you aren't, you can make up to the full deductible contribution if your family adjusted gross income is less than $176,000.

If you qualify for a SEP IRA, you can contribute up to 25 percent of your income to your retirement plan.

Once you've made the IRA contribution, your money can grow without taxes taking a bite from them. At 59½, you can start taking your money out—but you will pay income taxes on your withdrawals. Even if you don't need the money, you will be required to start taking some of it out after you turn 70½.

If you need any of the money before you are 59½, you may pay a steep 10 percent tax penalty on your withdrawals plus regular income tax.

THE DIRECT ROUTE

You can open either type of IRA at a brokerage firm, mutual fund, or bank, and can invest it in a number of possibilities, including mutual funds, stocks, bonds, real estate, or some collectibles. Your best bet for investing your IRA is to follow the advice for investing your 401(k) (see page 90) or that in "Beginning to Invest" (see page 219).

If you are young, a Roth IRA can be a great way to start saving for your later years. If you were to put an amount equal to your earnings from a summer or school job into a Roth IRA as a teenager or young adult, you'd have a big head start on your future.

If you're out of school and living on your own, of course, you first should have an emergency fund. And if you're working full time, you should contribute enough to an employer's 401(k) plan to get the matching contribution. (Never leave free money on the table!) If you still have money to save after that, consider at least some contribution to a Roth IRA. You'll have a long time for your money to compound, it can grow tax free, and you can have access to your contributions.

If you are young and don't have access to a retirement plan through a job, a Roth IRA is probably a better deal for you than a traditional IRA.

On the other hand, if you don't have a work retirement plan and make too much money to qualify for a Roth, a traditional IRA is the way to go. A traditional IRA also makes more sense if you think your tax rate now is higher than it is likely to be in retirement.

MANAGING AN INHERITANCE OR SETTLEMENT

Make the most of a windfall.

MAP IT

It seems far fetched, but it could happen: One day you could wake up and learn you've inherited an unexpected chunk of money from the estate of a loved one.

In a flash, you can see a million uses: a new car, a nice vacation, a chance to do something you always wanted to do. In your head, you'll probably spend it several times over.

Then reality hits. This may be the only time in your life that you get an opportunity to quickly change your financial situation. How you handle this windfall could make a difference for years to come.

DIRECTIONS

An inheritance rarely arrives in the form of a check. When a loved one dies, the person's life must be unraveled; closets must be emptied, bills must be paid, accounts and property transferred, and insurance collected. All of that can take time.

As a result, an inheritance is commonly paid over months, and sometimes years, and in the form of stocks, bonds, artwork, jewelry, and other property as well as cash. You may feel some responsibility to the deceased to manage the money the same way that he or she did or to keep the stuff you've inherited. The person may have even left instructions for you.

You'll also get a crash course in tax law. The federal government taxes estates depending on their sizes, though that is changing each year. In 2010, the estate tax is supposed to be eliminated—but only for one year. Then it is scheduled to return in 2011. The federal tax filing is due nine months after a person dies. States may also tax estates.

After those taxes are paid, you essentially start over. Any stocks, bonds, or other investments you inherit will usually be valued at their prices on the day the person died. In other words, assume your grandfather bought a stock thirty years ago. If you sell that stock after you inherit it, you will usually pay tax only on the difference between the sale price and the value on the day your grandfather died, not on the price he originally paid.

Tax-protected investments like Individual Retirement Accounts and 401(k)s have very specific rules about how much you can withdraw and how much tax you will have to pay. You should ask an accountant, investment professional, or lawyer before you touch any of the funds in the account, or you could face a whopping tax bill.

THE DIRECT ROUTE

The first thing you should do after receiving a big settlement or an inheritance is to sit tight and do nothing.

Before you start spending, you should take a while—several weeks to a few months, or more if necessary—to study the possibilities and develop a plan. Consult the administrator of any IRAs or 401(k)s to find out what your options are.

You may be itching to spend just a little of the money on a new car or to help out a friend or family member who has asked for a loan. But you'll make better use of that money if you take your time.

In the meantime, any cash should be invested in something safe, like an online savings account or money-market fund.

As you study your options, consider where your finances are strong and where they are weak. Do you have an emergency fund? Do you have any retirement savings? How much debt do you have? Do you own a house—or want to someday? All of those issues should be addressed before you consider a more ephemeral purchase like jewelry or a vacation.

Start to map out a plan. How much can you put away for the long term? How much debt would you like to pay down? Can you clean up your finances, put something away, and still have some money for something fun right now?

If you're going to put a big chunk toward reducing your debt, you should also commit to changing your habits so that you don't quickly run the bills back to where they were. Generally, you should pay off the most expensive debt first, starting with credit cards and your highest-interest loans.

This is now your money and you should feel free to invest it in ways that work for you rather than sticking to the investing style you inherited. If your grandfather owned municipal bonds and hated stocks, that was his choice. Probably, he needed the income in his old age. But that portfolio won't help you achieve your own financial goals and the money won't give you a boost if you don't put it in appropriate investments.

If the process seems too scary or feels overwhelming, seek out an adviser, like an accountant or a financial planner recommended by friends.

LIFE
INSURANCE

Extra protection for your loved ones.

MAP IT

Life insurance protects your family in case of your death by providing a sum of money to help cover what your paycheck used to provide. You may have coverage automatically through your company, and you can buy additional coverage from an insurance company.

Chances are that when you're just starting out, you won't really need life insurance, so we'll be brief here. As you age, however, you should consider buying a policy, even if you don't yet have a family. Life insurance is cheapest and most accessible when you're young and healthy, and it can be harder to acquire as you age and if you develop any health problems.

DIRECTIONS

Life insurance comes in two varieties, *term* and *cash value*. Term insurance covers you for a fixed amount over a certain term—one year, ten years, or more—at a relatively low cost. When the term is over and you stop paying, the insurance goes away.

Cash value insurance has a savings-account aspect to it and builds value. It is also much more expensive.

Life insurance primarily is intended to replace your income for those who rely on it. Most single people and most dual-earner couples without children don't have a burning need for it. However, if you provide support to parents, a sibling, spouse, or partner who doesn't work, you may want to buy insurance to replace that support. In addition, nonworking spouses with children should also have life insurance. If they were to die, the living spouse would need to pay for child care and other help.

When you apply for life insurance, you may be asked a series of personal questions, like your height and weight, whether you smoke cigarettes, how much alcohol you drink, and whether you have ever used illegal drugs. If you lie and are caught later, the policy could be invalidated, so you're better off telling the truth. You may also be asked to have a medical exam that includes having your blood taken.

Insurance companies use this information to set rates based on how risky they think it is to insure you. Even being slightly overweight or having minor health problems can result in a higher price, or premium, for insurance.

THE DIRECT ROUTE

While salespeople aggressively push cash-value insurance, there are many better investments out there. Stick with term insurance, and be sure to purchase a policy that is guaranteed to be renewed after your original term is up. That way you can keep the same policy as you age, although you will pay more for it.

How much insurance should you have? Experts recommend between five and twenty times the annual support you provide. Ten times that amount should be sufficient. So if you contribute $20,000 a year to a special-needs sibling, you should have $200,000 of coverage. If you already have some coverage through your job, you can buy a policy for the difference.

Although ten times your current support level may be a little more than you really need right now, it will give you some cushion if you are increasing your support over time, so that you don't have to keep raising your insurance. At some point, you may have children and a mortgage and will need much more insurance anyway. To get additional coverage, you may have to pass a medical exam and requalify.

Rates can vary, so shop around. Or, if you have already picked a reliable insurer for auto, renter's or homeowner's insurance, you may want the convenience of staying with one company.

In the event of your death, your life insurance, like your retirement accounts, will go to the beneficiary whom you designate with the insurance company no matter what your will might say. If you want everything to go to a significant other, but your parents are on the form, your significant other is out of luck. See the advice on choosing a beneficiary on page 102. If you marry, have children, or get divorced, you should update it. At the least, check it every presidential election year to make sure it's up to date.

Wills and Other Important Documents

Dealing with the inevitable.

MAP IT

It's a very sad fact, but someday you will die. When that happens, your family will have to deal with all that you've accumulated—your car, your clothes, your emergency savings, and your retirement account. One of the nicest things you can do for them is to let them know your wishes. And once you acquire any measurable assets, including a car or a home or savings of a few thousand dollars or more, you should have a will.

There's also a risk that illness or a severe accident could leave you unable to make decisions for yourself. So, once you turn eighteen, you should consider signing documents known as advance directives, which allow someone you trust to act on your behalf if you cannot.

Granted, this process is grim. But it can save the people who love you a lot of additional grief during an already difficult and emotional time.

DIRECTIONS

Once you're an adult, federal privacy laws may limit what doctors and hospitals can tell your parents and siblings and how much your family can control your care. There are several documents that might help you.

The Health Insurance Portability and Accountability Act of 1996, known as HIPAA, limits what doctors and nurses can say to your parents or siblings about your care without your permission. So when you fill out your doctor's paperwork, be sure to designate who else can ask questions or talk with a doctor on your behalf.

Depending on your state's laws and your preferences, you might need a health-care power of attorney, which gives someone the authority to make decisions for you if you can't make them yourself.

You might also need what is often called a living will, which speaks specifically to issues of prolonging life when your situation is irreversible. Think that's far fetched? Maybe, but several infamous battles over these life-or-death issues, including Terry Schiavo's, involved people who were impaired in their twenties.

On the financial side, you'll need to give someone your power of attorney so that your bills can be paid, your tax return filed, and other money matters can be cared for if you cannot do it.

If you die *intestate,* or without a will, state law will determine who gets what. Everything you own is part of your estate, including your pets. If you are single, all your assets may go to your parents, even if you'd rather they go to your siblings or cousins. If you have children, a judge could end up deciding who will raise them.

To really have a say in how your estate is handled, you need to have a will. In the will, you designate an executor who will unwind your estate according to your wishes.

THE DIRECT ROUTE

An estate lawyer may be able to draw up the appropriate advance directive documents for your state of residence for as little at $50 or $100. You can also find health-care documents on state Web sites or by state at www.CaringInfo.org. Another Web site, www.AgingWithDignity.org, sells a document called Five Wishes, which is recognized by forty states.

Hiring a lawyer to draw up a will as well as the advance-directive paperwork is likely to cost several hundred dollars to more than $1,000, depending on how complex your situation is. Though costly, a lawyer is also probably the most reliable way to go.

For very simple wills and estates, a software program will suffice. Just be aware that it probably won't address all the quirks in your state laws. Online programs are available through www.LegalZoom.com and www.Nolo.com, which also publishes Quicken WillMaker. Family Lawyer is another popular software package.

Once the will is drawn up, it must be signed by two witnesses who don't stand to inherit anything. In many states, the document doesn't need to be notarized, but it can be a good idea to do it anyway.

Finally, give copies of the documents to the key players—those who will make your health-care decisions, who will have power of attorney, and the executor. Keep a copy for yourself with your other important papers.

Every four or five years, or every presidential election year, if that's easier to remember, check to see if your state laws or personal circumstances have changed, and if so, update your documents.

GLOSSARY

Adjustable rate mortgage (ARM): A mortgage, or home loan, where the interest rate can go up or down every year or at another specified frequency, depending on interest rates in the broader economy. There is often a low "teaser" rate at the beginning, but the rate—and your mortgage payment—can climb dramatically in future years.

Adjusted gross income (AGI): An IRS calculation. AGI is your income, including your pay, dividends, and interest, minus items like interest on student loans and contributions to retirement accounts. Your AGI comes before the standard deduction or your itemized deductions are subtracted.

Advance Health Care Directive: Sometimes called an Advance Health Directive, this document (or documents depending on your state laws) lets your family and doctor know your health-care preferences in case you aren't in the physical or emotional shape to carry them out. These include designating who can make decisions for you if you are in an accident and might include your feelings about prolonging your life or whether you want to be an organ donor. A *living will* is a form of advance health directive.

Amortization schedule: A breakdown of the interest and principal paid with each payment on an installment loan. Initially, most of the payment goes to interest. By the end of the loan's term, most of the payment goes to principal.

Annual Percentage Rate (APR): The bottom-line interest rate charged on debt like credit cards and loans, allowing you to compare one offer to another. This number uses a standardized computation to take into account fees and costs and give you an actual annualized cost.

Annual Percentage Yield (APY): The interest paid over a full year's time on products such as bank accounts and certificates of deposit, allowing you to compare various offerings. The APY uses a standardized computation to take into account the effect of compounding, or the interest paid on your interest earned during the year.

Appreciation: An increase in value or price over time.

Assets: Items of value that can be converted into cash.

Automated teller machine (ATM): Machines owned by banks and others that dispense cash, take deposits, and handle other automated banking transactions.

Banks: These institutions take deposits for checking, savings, and other accounts, and put the money to work making loans to consumers for cars and homes and to businesses. Bank deposits are insured by the Federal Deposit Insurance Corporation up to specific limits.

Bankruptcy: The last-resort legal process for working out your debts.

Back-end load: A sales charge applied when you sell shares of certain mutual funds.

Basis point: $\frac{1}{100}$ of a percentage point. An increase of a quarter of a percentage point is the same as an increase of twenty-five basis points.

Bear market: A stock market when prices are generally falling. Some investment professionals define a bear market as one in which a broad measure of stocks, such as the Dow Jones Industrial Average, declines at least 20 percent.

Beneficiary: A person or entity designated to receive property or other assets from a will, retirement account, or insurance policy.

Big Board: Nickname for the New York Stock Exchange.

Bonds: Debt issued by companies or governments with a promise to repay the original amount plus specified interest by a specific date. Most bonds are issued in increments of $1,000 face value.

Bond ladder: A method of reducing your risk and increasing your yield with bond investments by buying bonds that mature in intervals. A bond ladder might include a bond that matures in two years, one that matures in four years, one in six years and one in eight years. When the first bond matures, it is replaced with a bond maturing in eight years, continuing the ladder.

Broker: A person or company that acts as a middleman in a transaction, helping you buy or sell stocks, real estate, or insurance for a commission or fee.

Bull market: A stock market when prices are generally rising.

Capital gains and losses: A gain or loss on the sale of an asset like stock or real estate bought as an investment. The government taxes capital gains on assets held for at least a year at a lower rate than regular income or short-term gains to encourage long-term investment and entrepreneurship.

Cash advance: Borrowing on your credit card to get cash. The credit card company will charge you a fee for using your credit card for a cash withdrawal and will charge interest until the advance is paid back. This is an expensive way to get cash that should be used only in emergency situations.

Certificate of deposit (CD): A type of account that pays a fixed interest rate if you agree to leave your money alone for a certain period of time. These are issued by banks and insured by the Federal Deposit Insurance Corporation. You can buy CDs with maturities from one month to five years or longer. However, if you need your money before the CD matures, you will probably pay a penalty for withdrawing it.

COBRA: The Consolidated Omnibus Budget Reconciliation Act gives workers and their families the right to extend their health insurance for a period of time after a job loss, death, divorce, or other life events. While maintaining health-care coverage, individuals typically pay more for health insurance under COBRA than they paid to their employer because they bear the full cost of the premium.

Consolidation: With student loans, it's the combination of all your loans into one new loan.

Contract: A legally binding agreement.

Copayment: The portion of a medical bill that the insurance company requires you to pay when you visit the doctor. Also called *copay.*

Coupon rate: In a bond, this is the interest rate paid each year. A bond with a coupon of 5 percent pays $50 in interest for each $1,000 of face value, usually in two installments.

Credit card: A popular form of high-cost debt. Credit cards allow you to borrow money and pay back all or part of your borrowings each month. For that privilege, you pay a high rate of interest on borrowings that you don't repay each month.

Credit limit: The maximum amount you can borrow on your credit card. If you exceed the limit, you'll pay a fee in addition to the interest you'll pay on your borrowings.

Credit score: A numerical grade that aims to tell lenders how likely you are to repay your debts. Your credit score is based on your past payment record, how much you borrow, how long you've been borrowing, and other factors. The best known is the FICO score developed by Fair Isaac Corporation (see also *FICO score*).

Credit union: A financial cooperative owned by its members that acts much like a bank. Credit unions offer checking and savings accounts and car loans. Accounts there are insured. Often credit unions will offer lower interest rates on loans and better options on savings accounts than regular banks.

Debit card: A card that looks like a credit card but works more like a personal check. When you use a debit card, whether to withdraw money from an ATM or make purchases, the funds are withdrawn from your bank account right away. When you make a purchase, you can either put in your personal identification number (PIN) or sign a receipt as you would with a credit card. Debit cards can be more convenient than using cash, but they have fewer protections than credit cards.

Deductible: In insurance, the amount you must pay before your insurance kicks in. For instance, if your car sustains $2,000 in damage and your deductible is $500, you will pay $500 and the insurance company will pay $1,500. With health insurance, you must meet the deductible each year before insurance will pay its part; with car, homeowners, or renter's insurance, the deductible applies to each claim you make. Generally, the higher a deductible you're willing to pay, the less your insurance will cost.

Deductions: Items that help reduce the income tax you owe by reducing your taxable income. Depending on their size and your income, mortgage interest, charitable contributions, and property taxes can be tax deductions that trim the income taxes you pay.

Dependent care account: An opportunity for working parents to put away pretax dollars toward child care for youngsters under thirteen years old. Offered through employers, these plans allow you to put up to $5,000 per family into an account before taxes and then use the funds to pay for day care centers, nannies, or day camps.

Direct deposit: The electronic deposit of your paycheck directly into your account, replacing a paper check that is physically deposited. The IRS may also directly deposit your income-tax refund in your bank account.

Diversification: Choosing a variety of different investments to reduce your risk while maintaining or improving your return. Diversification usually helps minimize the ups and downs of investing.

Dollar-cost averaging: The process of investing a fixed amount regularly over time regardless of the price. Dollar-cost averaging smooths out the highs and lows and eliminates worries about buying at a high point.

Dow Jones Industrial Average (DJIA): An average of thirty industrial stocks that serves as a representation of the broader stock market. When the guy on TV says the market was up or down, he is usually referring to the performance of the Dow Jones average that day.

Down payment: An initial cash payment on a large purchase. With a car or home, the rest of the amount owed is financed through a loan that is repaid over time.

Earnings per share: How much profit a company earns for each share of stock it has outstanding. The earnings per share is calculated by dividing the quarterly or annual net income by the number of shares outstanding.

Equity: Ownership. In real estate, your equity is the portion of the property that is yours after the debt is subtracted. If you own a $400,000 home with a $300,000 mortgage, your equity is $100,000. In investing, stocks are often called *equities*.

Escrow: Money or property put into the hands of a third party until certain conditions are met. For instance, when you make a deposit on a property purchase, your initial deposit may be held in escrow until you close the deal. In addition, your mortgage company may collect monthly payments on property taxes and homeowner's insurance and hold on to them until those annual payments are due.

Estate: All the things you own that have value. Estate planning refers to planning for how your assets will be distributed at your death.

Exchange-traded fund (ETF): A type of investment that acts like an index mutual fund but trades like a stock. Exchange-traded funds often mimic an index like the Standard & Poor's 500. But unlike an index mutual fund, the price fluctuates during the day and the ETFs can be bought and sold at any time.

Expense ratio: A mutual fund's cost of doing business, stated as a percentage of its assets. Operating expenses are subtracted from fund assets and reduce the investment returns earned by fund shareholders.

Face value: In bonds, the amount of the original bond and the amount paid when the bond comes due, usually $1,000. The face value is also known as the *par value.*

Free Application for Federal Student Aid (FAFSA): The form that you need to fill out if you're interested in financial aid to help with college costs.

FICA: On your paycheck, the money subtracted to pay for Social Security and Medicare may be labeled FICA. That's short for the Federal Insurance Contributions Act, which calls for a portion of an individual's pay to go to Social Security and Medicare. In 2009, 12.4 percent of a person's salary of up to $106,800 will go to Social Security and 2.9 percent of pay (without a dollar cap) will go to Medicare. The employee pays half and the employer pays the other half. If you are self-employed, you'll pay the full 15.3 percent, though half of the amount will be deductible as a business expense.

FICO score: A credit score developed by Fair Isaac Corporation based on your debt, payment history, and other factors that is intended to measure how likely you are to repay a loan. Lenders look to this score to assess how risky it would be to loan money to you.

Fiduciary: A person who manages assets for the benefit of someone else and who is required to put that person's interests above his or her own. Directors of a company have a fiduciary duty to the company's shareholders; lawyers have a fiduciary duty to their clients. Real-estate brokers have a fiduciary duty to the seller of a property, but often not to the buyer. However, some financial advisers act as fiduciaries and others do not. Before you turn over funds to a broker or adviser or hire someone to represent you, ask if the relationship includes a fiduciary duty to act in your best benefit.

Fixed-income investments: Investments that return income at regular, fixed intervals, like savings accounts, certificates of deposit, and bonds.

Fixed-rate mortgage: A home loan with an interest rate and monthly payment that will stay the same over the life of the loan. Most fixed-rate mortgages are for either thirty-year or fifteen-year terms.

Flexible spending account: A work benefit that allows you to use pretax income to help pay for child-care or medical expenses. Once a year, your employer will give you the opportunity to determine how much you want to contribute to this account before income taxes, Social Security, and Medicare, up to certain maximums. These accounts have a use-it-or-lose-it feature. If you don't spend all that you put away over a calendar year (and, sometimes, a short grace period after the year ends), you will lose the money.

Float: In stocks, the float is the stock that is available for trading by the public, or the amount that isn't held by insiders. In banking, the float is the time between a transaction and when it hits your bank account, such as the delay between when you write a check and when the dollars are subtracted from your account.

401(k) plan: Named for the provision of the tax code that allowed retirement contributions to be made before taxes, these company-sponsored plans allow you to make pretax contributions toward your retirement and allow the investments to grow tax-deferred until you reach retirement age. If you withdraw your investments early, you will pay a steep tax penalty. When you withdraw them during retirement, the funds will be taxed as income.

Foreclosure: The process where a bank or other lender takes possession of a home after the homeowner has failed to keep up with mortgage or home-equity-loan payments. The lender can then sell the home to someone else to recoup all or part of the loan.

Front-end load: An up-front sales charge applied when you buy shares of certain mutual funds.

Grace period: With credit cards, the period between the end of a monthly billing period and when the bill is due, typically two or three weeks. If you pay your entire bill every month, you won't pay interest during the grace period; if you carry a balance, you will pay interest on the balance and new charges and won't benefit from the grace period. With student loans, the grace period is the time between the end of school and when you start paying off the loan.

Gross income: All of your income from work, investments, and other sources before any taxes or deductions.

Growth stocks: Stocks of companies whose profits are expected to grow much faster than average. Buyers hope that growth will translate into above-average increases in the stock price.

Health savings account: An account designed to help those with health-care plans that have high deductibles. You can contribute pretax dollars to this account, and money in the account can grow tax-free. The funds can be used to pay for medical expenses. Unlike a flexible spending account, these funds can be carried over from year to year.

Hedge funds: Lightly regulated investment pools aimed at big wealthy investors (like universities and pension funds) that may use strategies like borrowing, mathematical models, or bets against certain stocks to try to generate above-average investment returns. Hedge funds usually require a large minimum investment and charge relatively steep fees.

Income tax: A government tax on your income. In the United States, those with income above a certain minimum must file an income tax form every year.

Index mutual fund: A mutual fund that tracks a specific stock or bond index, such as the Standard & Poor's 500 Stock Index of 500 large stocks. Typically, these funds have low expenses.

Individual Retirement Account (IRA): A tax-favored account for retirement savings that you establish outside of your employer. Individuals who don't have other retirement plans or who meet income requirements can make tax-deductible contributions to these accounts, which grow tax-deferred. See also Roth IRAs.

Inflation: The rate at which prices of goods and services rise, reducing your purchasing power. The most common measure of inflation is the change in the government's consumer price index, or CPI, which is reported monthly.

Initial public offering (IPO): A company's first sale of stock to the public.

Insufficient funds: A term used when a person writes a check or uses a debit card to take out more money than is in his or her checking account. Banks often charge fees for checks that are returned for insufficient funds. Sometimes called *NSF,* or non-sufficient funds.

Interest: The amount paid for using someone else's money. Savings accounts and bonds pay interest for the right to have access to your money. You pay interest when you borrow money.

Interest rate: The annual percentage to be paid on the amount originally borrowed. A savings account may pay from less than 1 percent to 5 percent interest per year, or less than $1 to $5 for each $100 saved. A credit card may charge 17 percent or more interest a year on your balances, or $17 or more for each $100 owed.

Intestate: A person who dies without a legal will. State laws spell out how assets are to be distributed in these situations.

Invoice price: With cars, roughly what the dealer paid for the car.

Itemized deductions: If your total tax deductions are greater than the standard deduction allowed by the Internal Revenue Service, you can itemize or list them on Form 1040. Itemizing deductions can reduce your overall income tax bill.

Jumbo mortgage: A mortgage loan above a certain limit, which ranged from $417,000 to $729,750 in 2008, depending on location. In 2009, the top limit is scheduled to decline to $625,500. Generally, the interest rates on jumbo loans are higher than for conventional mortgages.

Junk bond: A bond that is considered too risky to be investment grade. Bonds rated BB or lower by Standard & Poor's or Ba or lower by Moody's are considered to be speculative or *junk* bonds.

Keogh plan: A type of retirement plan for self-employed people or entities that aren't incorporated.

Large-cap stock: Generally speaking, a company with a market capitalization—or a stock market value—of $10 billion or more.

Lease: A long-term rental agreement sealed with a contract that specifies the terms.

Liabilities: Debts and other financial obligations. The opposite of assets.

Life-cycle funds: Diversified mutual funds that may own stocks, bonds, and cash in a mix aimed at the long term. The funds may aim toward a specific retirement date or may be designated as aggressive, moderate, or conservative in their investing. These funds are intended to give investors one simple option for retirement investing.

Liquidity: The ability to pay your bills with cash on hand or to convert your assets to cash quickly. Because most stocks trade daily, they are very liquid. Investments in art or real estate, however, are less liquid because they can be difficult and time-consuming to sell.

Manufacturer's suggested retail price (MSRP): In car-buying, the suggested selling price or the sticker price on a car, which includes profits for the car dealer and the manufacturer. This price doesn't include taxes, registration costs, and other fees. Typically, there is room to negotiate a price below the MSRP.

Market cap: A company's stock-market value, measured by multiplying its stock price times the number of shares it has outstanding. Market cap is short for *market capitalization.*

Maturity: When a security such as a bond comes due or is to be paid in full.

Medicare: The federal health insurance program for the disabled and for people who are at least sixty-five years old.

Midcap stock: Generally speaking, a company with a market capitalization—or a stock market value—of $2 billion to $10 billion.

Minimum payment due: The minimum amount you must pay to stay current with your monthly credit card bill. Generally, this is a very small percentage of what you owe, and you should ignore the number and pay off the bill or pay as much as you possibly can each month to avoid steep interest charges.

Money-market account: A kind of savings account typically offered by banks and credit unions. Money-market accounts often pay higher interest rates than regular savings accounts, but also require larger balances. They are insured by the FDIC up to $250,000.

Money-market mutual fund: A mutual fund that invests in very short-term, highly liquid securities and aims to maintain a constant price of $1 a share. Money-market mutual funds are not currently insured but are considered fairly low risk.

Money order: A check that may be purchased for a fee at a store, bank, or post office that allows one person to pay money to another. Because the amount of the money order is paid at the time of purchase, recipients usually consider money orders more reliable than a personal check.

Mortgage: A home loan or other real-estate loan.

Municipal bonds: Debt issued by a state, county, or local government. Also known as *munis*. Interest is usually exempt from federal income tax and also from state tax in the state where it was issued.

Mutual fund: A professionally managed pool of money funded by a number of investors. Mutual fund managers may buy stocks, bonds, or other securities based on the fund's goals and objectives for the benefit of the whole group.

Nasdaq Stock Market: An electronic stock market that is home to many technology stocks. The acronym once stood for the National Association of Securities Dealers Automated Quotation.

Net worth: Your assets, including all your investments, bank accounts, and items of value, minus your liabilities, including your debts.

Network, health care: Doctors, hospitals, and other health-care providers that have signed contracts with your health insurance company to provide services at certain prices. Generally, your insurance company will reimburse you more for in-network providers than for those that aren't part of the network.

New York Stock Exchange: The oldest and most prestigious stock exchange in the U.S., sometimes called the Big Board.

No-haggle dealers: Car dealers who sell their cars at a set price, eliminating the traditional haggling process over what you will pay. Buyers still negotiate their financing and the value of the trade-in, however, which may ultimately affect the end price of the car.

No-load fund: A mutual fund without a commission or sales charge.

OASDI: Old Age, Survivors, and Disability Insurance program. The official name for Social Security.

Out-of-pocket maximum: In health insurance, this is the maximum amount you'll have to pay for health care in a given year. After you have paid deductibles, copays, and your portion of medical expenses up to your out-of-pocket maximum, your health insurance should pick up the rest of the bills.

Overdraft: When you write checks or make payments with your debit card that exceed the amount of money that you have in your account, resulting in a negative balance—also known as bouncing a check. When this happens, your account is *overdrawn* and the bank has the option to pay or not pay the amount. If it does pay, it will probably charge you fees that must be paid in addition to repaying the overdraft amount. You may also have to pay fees to the store or company that received the bounced check, and your credit record may be scarred.

Overdraft protection: A bank service where the bank agrees to loan you the money to cover your overdrafts up to a certain amount. Some banks charge for protection itself; some just charge if you overdraw your account. You can also link your savings account or credit card to your checking account so that funds are taken from one of those if you overdraw your account. You'll still pay fees, but they will likely be smaller than if you didn't have a back-up option.

Par value: The face value of a bond, usually $1,000.

Payday loan: An expensive, short-term loan of two weeks to a month intended to provide cash until the next paycheck. Payday loans are typically less than $500 and charge very high interest rates.

Personal Identification Number (PIN): Your personal secret password that gives you access to ATMs, online accounts, and other password-protected accounts.

Phishing: Using a fake Web site, pop-up advertisement, or e-mail that looks legitimate to extract personal information or account information from unsuspecting victims.

Points: In home-buying, one point equals 1 percent of the amount borrowed. Points are up-front fees assessed to lower your mortgage interest rate or fees required to close the loan.

Typically, it takes five years or more to recoup the savings from paying a point to secure a lower interest rate. In bond prices, a point is 1 percent of the bond's face value, or $10 for every $1,000 face value. In stocks, a point is $1; a stock that's up three points is up $3.

Portfolio: Your holdings of stocks, bonds, and other investments. A diversified portfolio will have a mix of investments.

Pre-existing condition: A medical ailment that existed before you signed up for your health insurance. Group health insurance may exclude coverage for pre-existing conditions for no longer than eighteen months. How individual policies treat pre-existing conditions depends on your state's laws.

Premium: In insurance, the amount you pay the insurance company for your coverage. Premiums may be paid monthly, once a year, or on different payment schedules. With bonds, a premium is the amount you pay for the bond above the face value. When current interest rates are lower than a bond's coupon rate, the bond may trade at a premium to its face value.

Preferred stock: A kind of stock that typically pays a fixed dividend. Preferred shares tend to trade based on their dividend yield, more like a bond. But unlike a bond, preferred stock doesn't come with a maturity date. Companies must pay the dividend on preferred shares before they pay dividends on common shares.

Prepaid card: Gift cards, Starbucks cards, and other plastic cards where money is loaded first, allowing you to spend it when you're ready. Unlike a credit card, you can't spend more than is on a prepaid card. Some cards can be reloaded and some companies will replace a card that you have registered if the card is lost or stolen. Some card issuers may charge fees when you add money to your card or when you use it—or if you don't use it for a long time.

Price-to-earnings ratio (P/E ratio): A measure of how a stock is valued by the market. The P/E ratio reflects how much investors are willing to pay for each $1 of company's profits. The P/E is calculated by dividing a company's current stock price by its most recent four quarters of earnings per share. A *forward P/E* is calculated by dividing the current stock price by the expected earnings per share over the next year. Sometimes called a stock's *earnings multiple.*

Primary care physician (PCP): Your main doctor, who acts as the point person for health-insurance purposes. Some health-insurance plans require you to see your primary care physician first or to get a referral from that doctor before you can see a specialist.

Principal: In a loan, the actual amount you borrowed. With an installment loan like a mortgage, your regular payment covers primarily interest charges at the beginning and primarily the principal at the end.

Prospectus: A legal document that spells out the terms of a security being sold to the public. The prospectus should give you enough relevant information to make an informed decision. Before you buy a mutual fund, you must be given a prospectus that outlines the fund's goals and objectives, management, and fees.

Quote: The most recent price for a stock or bond. Also known as the *quoted price.*

Rebalancing: The process of periodically transferring money within your portfolio so that it meets your asset-allocation goals.

Because one sector of the market may outperform another, you may want to bring your portfolio back into balance once or twice a year by rebalancing your investment mix.

Replacement cost coverage: Insurance coverage that will pay you enough to actually replace possessions that have been damaged or destroyed, rather than reimbursing you for their recent market price.

Roth 401(k): An employer-sponsored retirement-savings account funded with money on which you have already paid taxes. Once invested, the funds can grow tax-free and are tax-free when they are withdrawn at retirement. This investment makes sense for people who think they may be in a higher tax bracket in retirement than they are now.

Roth Individual Retirement Account (Roth IRA): A kind of retirement account funded with after-tax dollars that then grows tax-free. Withdrawals at retirement are also tax-free. The principal can be withdrawn tax-free at any time.

Rule of 72: The mathematical rule for figuring out how long it will take to double your money. Divide your expected interest rate or return into 72. For example, investments with an average return of 8 percent will double every nine years. To double your money every ten years, you need to average a 7.2 percent return.

Russell 2000 Index: An index of 2,000 small-company stocks. The Russell 2000 is a widely followed benchmark for the small-cap company universe.

Savings account: An easily accessible account at a bank or credit union that pays a modest interest rate on your savings.

Secured credit card: A credit card backed by a deposit in a bank account. The available credit on the card is limited by the amount in the account. Secured cards are designed for people with no credit record or a poor one and can help those individuals rebuild or establish a credit history.

Securities firms: Also called brokerages or broker-dealers, these companies buy and sell stocks, bonds, and other investments on behalf of their customers and themselves.

Short-selling: A bet that a stock price will go down. Short-sellers borrow stock from brokerage firms and sell it, with the goal of buying it back at a lower price.

Simplified Employee Pension (SEP-IRA): A kind of retirement plan for the self-employed and for those at companies without retirement plans. Contributions to a SEP-IRA are tax-deductible. Investments grow tax-deferred and you will pay taxes when you withdraw the funds at retirement.

Small-cap stock: Generally speaking, a company with a market capitalization—or a stock market value—of between $300 million and $2 billion.

Social Security: The government program that provides retirement and disability income.

Standard & Poor's 500 Stock Index: An index of 500 large-cap U.S. stocks that is considered a benchmark for the stock market.

Standard deduction: A deduction available to all taxpayers that reduces the amount on which you pay federal income taxes. The size of the deduction depends on whether you are married and how many people are in your household, among other things. The standard deduction applies only to people who don't itemize their tax deductions.

Stock: A kind of security that reflects ownership in a company. Also called equity or shares. Over the long term, stock ownership has outperformed other investments.

Stock option: The right to buy a stock at a specific price up to a certain date. Companies issue stock options as a way to compensate executives and others and as a way to encourage managers and employees to think like stockholders.

Strike price: The price at which a stock option can be exercised. Also called the exercise price. If your company grants you options to buy 100 shares at $50 a share, then your strike price is $50. You would exercise the option only if the current price is above the strike price.

Sublet: A side agreement in which you lease your apartment to someone else but still remain on the lease and responsible for the property. For example, if you take a summer job in another location, you may want to sublet your place so that someone else pays all or part of the rent while you're away. However, since you are the person leasing, you are still on the hook for the rent and any damage to the property.

Target date mutual fund: A mutual fund that is structured with a specific retirement date in mind, such as a 2050 fund. The fund will own a mix of stocks, bonds, and cash and will be more aggressive in the early years and more conservative as the target date draws near. Also known as *life-cycle funds*.

Tax deferral: A delay in taxation until funds are actually withdrawn. Then, the withdrawals are taxed. Individual retirement accounts and 401(k)s grow tax-deferred, but are taxed when the retiree taps them.

Tax free: Not subject to current or future tax consequences. Contributions to Roth IRAs are made after taxes, and both the growth and the withdrawals are tax free. The interest on municipal bonds is generally free from federal income tax and state taxes in the state where they are issued.

Teaser rate: An initial, temporary rate intended to entice you to sign up for a credit card or other loan or to open an interest-bearing account. Typically, the rate changes after three or six months to one that's less attractive.

1040: One of the primary forms for filing federal income taxes. Some taxpayers can file using the simpler 1040EZ or 1040A.

Term life insurance: Pure life insurance that provides coverage over a set period of time. When the policy is up, you have a choice of renewing it or letting it lapse. By contrast, *cash value life insurance* has an investment component as well as life insurance.

Thrifts: Financial institutions such as savings banks and savings & loans.

Treasuries: Securities sold by the U.S. Treasury to meet government expenses. Treasury bills mature within one year, Treasury notes mature within one to ten years, and Treasury bonds mature in more than ten years. Treasury notes and bonds are sold in denominations of $100 and pay interest twice a year.

Underwater or Upside down: Terms used to describe a situation where you owe more on something than it is now worth. If your home price drops below what you owe on your mortgage or your car loan is for more than the value of your car, you are said to be underwater or upside down.

Value stock: A stock believed to have greater potential than its current price indicates. Investors see value stocks as bargains that are undervalued relative to their real worth.

Variable interest rate: An interest rate that can change. Many variable interest rates are tied to changes in benchmarks, such as the U.S. prime rate or the London Interbank Offer Rate, the LIBOR.

Vesting: The process under which employees receive benefits over a period of time. Stock options that are granted typically vest over three or four years; a three-year vesting period means you'll take ownership of one-third the first year, two-thirds the second year and all of them the third year. Companies may require five or more years of service before you are vested in a pension plan, or before you are vested in your 401(k) match.

W-2 form: The form your employer sends to you and the IRS every year showing what you earned and how much was withheld for taxes.

W-4 form: The form you fill out when you start a new job that determines how much of your pay is withheld for income taxes. You can file a new W-4 to increase or decrease your withholding at any time.

Withholding: Taxes taken out of your income before you actually receive your paycheck.

Yield: The percentage return on an investment or loan. A $100 investment that pays $5 a year in interest has a yield of 5 percent. Financial companies use standard methods in quoting the yields on bank accounts, money-market funds, and bonds.

Yield to maturity: The yield, or percentage return, received if you hold a bond until it matures. The yield-to-maturity is one of the most widely quoted yields for bonds.

HELPFUL WEB SITES

The Internet is amazing in its breadth and depth, and also in its ability to make a sales pitch seem innocent and inviting. Sorting between the thorough and useful and the naked attempt to sell you a service can be challenging, and sometimes the two can't be separated. For instance, both the credit card and cell phone Web sites below are likely to be paid if you click on a link that takes you to a service provider.

The links below are in no way comprehensive. Any company worth doing financial business with today will have its own site, but there are way too many to list them here. Still, you will benefit by checking out a company's specific services yourself.

The listing below isn't intended as an endorsement of any site or service. Rather, it's an attempt to help you cut through the online clutter and quickly get the information you need most.

BANK RATES

Sites that list good deals on checking accounts, savings accounts, and money-market accounts

www.BankingMyWay.com

www.Bankrate.com, the best of the bunch

www.Banx.com

BUDGETING

Weigh your goals and keep track of your spending

www.Geezeo.com, an online, social-networking site

www.Microsoft.com/money, online version of popular software

www.Mint.com, a powerful, free online tool

/money.CNN.com/magazines/moneymag/money101/ lesson1/ for a priority analyzer

www.Quicken.intuit.com, online version of popular software

www.Wesabe.com, an online site

www.WSJ.com/booktools, a simple but useful tool

CAR BUYING

Information about cars, reviews, car prices, negotiating suggestions, and other tips

www.Autos.yahoo.com, Yahoo!'s car site

www.Cars.com, broad car site

www.CarFax.com, service that will check a used vehicle's history

www.CarTalk.com, the site of the popular public radio show

www.ConsumerReports.org, well-known for its thorough car testing, requires subscription

www.Edmunds.com, a top site for seeing what others are paying for new cars www.IISH.org/ratings, the Insurance Institute for Highway Safety car crash ratings

www.JDPower.com, also known for its testing

www.KBB.com (for Kelley Blue Book), a top site for car pricing

www.NADA.com, the National Association of Auto Dealers

www.Safercar.gov, the U.S. government's auto-crash ratings

CELL PHONES

Compare services and pricing, check out equipment and reviews

www.CNET.org, lots of product reviews

www.ConsumerReports.org, rates service providers, requires subscription

www.JDPower.com, also offers ratings

www.LetsTalk.com, for comparing products

www.MyRatePlan.com, for comparing services, phones and plans

www.PhoneDog.com, for comparing services, phones and plans

www.PhoneScoop.com, for reviews and products

CHARITIES

Check them out before you give

www.CharityNavigator.org

www.Dmachoice.org (to cut down on junk mail)

www.Give.org

www.Guidestar.org

CREDIT CARDS

Places to compare offerings, interest rates and other terms

www.Bankrate.com

www.Cardtrak.com, comparison shopping site

www.Cardratings.com, comparison shopping site

www.Credit.com, site with advice and card insight

www.FederalReserve.gov/pubs/shop, Federal Reserve information on choosing a card

www.CCCServices.com, Consumer Credit Counseling Services

www.NFCC.org, National Foundation for Credit Counseling

CREDIT REPORTS AND SCORES

Understanding your credit rating and finding out more about your credit reports

www.AnnualCreditReport.com, the site for getting your free credit report from the big three credit reporting services

(Note that www.freecreditreport.com, which advertises on television, is a commercial service, not the site for getting your free once-a-year credit report)

www.Experian.com, a credit-reporting service

www.Equifax.com, a credit-reporting service

www.Transunion.com, a credit-reporting service

www.MyFico.com, the consumer site from Fair Isaac Corporation, the creator of the FICO score

FINANCIAL EDUCATION

Sites that explain how the system works and offer tips for navigating it

www.Consumer.gov, a government consumer site

www.Consumer-action.org, a consumer advocacy site, most useful for its publications

www.ConsumerFed.org, a consumer advocacy site

www.ConsumerJungle.org, a site aimed at students and teachers

www.FederalReserveEducation.org, education site of the Federal Reserve

www.FINRA.org, the site for the Financial Industry Regulatory Authority, formerly the National Association of Securities Dealers, the non-governmental regulator of securities firms

www.MyMoney.gov, from the U.S. Financial Literacy and Education Commission

www.SaveandInvest.org, a FINRA investor education site

www.SEC.gov/investor, the Securities and Exchange Commission investor site

www.USPIRG.org, the site of the U.S. Public Interest Research Group, a top consumer advocate. State PIRGs also have their own sites

FINANCIAL INFORMATION

Where to go for advice, explanation, helpful calculators, and insight on a huge range of financial topics

www.About.com/money, site where guides offer expert advice

www.Finance.aol.com, AOL's financial site

www.Finance.yahoo.com, Yahoo!'s financial site

www.Kiplinger.com, access to many informative and useful articles

www.MarketWatch.com, a good consumer investing site

Money.cnn.com, *Money* magazine's site

www.SmartMoney.com, a thorough site with lots of helpful information

www.WSJ.com, *The Wall Street Journal* site, some of which requires a subscription

INSURANCE INFORMATION

Sites for searching insurance rates and learning more about the business

www.AccuCoverage.com, homeowner's insurance site

www.AccuQuote.com, an insurance shopping site

www.eHealthInsurance.com, health-insurance shopping site

www.FloodSmart.gov, the U.S. government's flood insurance site

www.III.org, site of the Insurance Information Institute, a group supported by the insurance industry

www.Insure.com, an insurance shopping site

www.InsWeb.com, auto-insurance shopping site

www.knowyourstuff.org, home inventory software

www.LifeHappens.org, a life-insurance education site with calculators

www.USAAEdFoundation.org, a nonprofit arm of the insurer aimed at education

INVESTING INFORMATION

Sources for more specific information on various kinds of investments

Apps.finra.org/Investor_Information/EA/1/mfetf.aspx, or www.FINRA.org, then click "Investors" and "Tools & Calculators" to get to FINRA's analyzer for mutual funds and exchange traded funds and their expenses

www.ETFConnect.com, a Nuveen Investments site that has a wealth of information on ETFs

www.FINRA.org/InvestorInformation/ToolsCalculators/index.htm, FINRA calculators

401k.fidelity.com, information about retirement savings from a mutual-fund firm

www.HSH.com, a thorough mortgage-tracking site

www.ICI.org/funds, an investor section of the Investment Company Institute, the mutual-fund industry's trade group, which has many links to other financial sites

www.iMoneyNet.com, where to find money-market mutual fund rates

www.Morningstar.com, the top site for researching mutual funds and stocks and comparing fund costs. Using some of the best services requires a subscription

www.TreasuryDirect.gov, the U.S. Treasury's site for buying government notes and bonds directly

www.WSJ.com, the market data section has fund screeners and other useful tools and information

STUDENT LOANS AND FINANCIAL AID

Starting points for financing your education

www.CollegeAnswer.com, the education site for a large student-loan lender

www.CollegeBoard.com, look for the *Pay for College* section

www.FAFSA.gov, the site for the crucial financial-aid form

www.FastWeb.com, comprehensive scholarship information

www.FinAid.org, a very comprehensive financial-aid site

www.LoanConsolidation.ed.gov, the government site for student-loan consolidation

www.MyRichUncle.com, helps find deals on student loans

www.SimpleTuition.com, site for comparing lenders

www.StudentAid.ed.gov, a government site for financial aid

TAXES

Where to find the basics

www.Fool.com/taxes, articles on lots of tax issues

www.IRS.gov, the Internal Revenue Service site

www.PaycheckCity.com, paycheck calculators

TRAVEL

Some of the many sites to help you find a way to your vacation hotspots

www.FareCompare.com, shows the lowest recent fare for a route

www.Expedia.com, major travel-shopping site

www.Hotels.com, the name sums it up

www.Kayak.com, site that pulls information from a number of different travel sites

www.Orbitz.com, major travel-shopping site

www.STAtravel.com, a student-travel site

www.StudentUniverse.com, a student-travel site

www.Travelocity.com, major travel-shopping site

www.TSA.gov, the Transportation Security Administration site

www.Mobissimo.com, a travel search engine

WILLS AND ESTATES

Starting points for end-of-life issues

www.AgingWithDignity.org, home of a Five Wishes document to guide your family if you can't make decisions yourself

www.Caringinfo.org, site with links to state-specific living wills and advance directives

www.LegalZoom.com, will-making software

www.Nolo.com, will-making software

ACKNOWLEDGMENTS

Special thanks go to the many people who helped out with details, listened to theories, and offered guidance and expert advice on these many subjects, especially Jennifer Altabef; Neal Boudette and Anne Marie Chaker of *The Wall Street Journal;* Dan Culloton of Morningstar; Sheila Curran of Duke University's Career Center; Mark Kantrowitz of FinAid.org; Warner May of AT&T; Greg McBride of Bankrate.com; Kirk Parsons of J.D. Power; Anna Post of the Emily Post Institute; Sol S. Reifer of Wright Ginsberg Brusilow; Jill Risman; Kate Seguin of Ohio State; Susan Seiter of Smith Barney; Jodi Smith of Mannersmith; Craig Watts of Fair Isaac; and John Woerth of Vanguard.

Karen Damato was a thorough and insightful reader whose enormous knowledge of personal finance improved many of these pages. I am also grateful to Saralynn Busch, Joan Gass and Patricia Hinton, who took the time to read early manuscripts and offer suggestions.

Rose Ellen D'Angelo at *The Wall Street Journal* and John Mahaney at Crown got behind this idea early on and were both endlessly supportive. Lindsay Orman was an unflappable, patient and thoughtful editor. Andrea Peabbles's careful and smart copyediting cleaned up the text. Siri Silleck, Lauren Dong, and Jie Yang helped make this accessible to a different kind of *Wall Street Journal* audience and Karen Miller Pensiero at *The Wall Street Journal* helped tie up loose ends.

My daughters Abby and Jenny inspired this effort, challenged ideas, and gave their honest feedback. My husband, Scott McCartney, shared his amazing knowledge of the travel business, and then put up with my obsessions and read many drafts. The seed for this project was planted at home, with a sharp exchange with a teenager who shook a checkbook register at me, and demanded, "Why do I need this?"

Such a simple question. Such a long answer.

INDEX

ABOUT THE AUTHOR

Karen Blumenthal writes the Family Money column for *The Wall Street Journal* and has been a financial journalist for more than twenty-five years.

She has written about a wide range of financial and corporate subjects and is the author of *Grande Expectations: A Year in the Life of Starbucks' Stock*. She has also written two award-winning nonfiction books for young people.

As an author, she has appeared on *ABC World News Tonight*, the *Today Show*, and the *PBS Nightly Business Report*. *Kiplinger's* magazine named *Grande Expectations* one of the five best investing reads of 2007.

The Wall Street Journal
SPECIAL OFFER

The One Investment You Can Count On.

2 WEEKS FREE!

YES! Send me **2 FREE WEEKS** of The Wall Street Journal and also enter my subscription for an additional 26 weeks at the money-saving rate of only $49.00 — just 32¢ a day! I receive 28 weeks in all and **SAVE 65%** off the regular rate.

Order now! ▶

Name

Address

City

State   Zip

2PCJM

DOWJONES

CALL NOW FOR FASTER SERVICE!
1-800-620-5798

THE WALL STREET JOURNAL.

The Guide in your hands is a great way to start building wealth.

The best way to <u>keep your assets growing</u> is to read THE WALL STREET JOURNAL!

Send in the card below and receive

2 WEEKS FREE